An Interview With
THE DALAI LAMA

By John F. Avedon

LITTLEBIRD PUBLICATIONS

PHOTOGRAPHS BY RICHARD AVEDON

DESIGN AND PRODUCTION BY ELIZABETH AVEDON

Littlebird Publications
126 Fifth Avenue   New York, 10011

Printed in the United States of America
Second Printing

Copyright © 1980 by John F. Avedon
All rights reserved.

Library of Congress Catalog Card No.: 80-83015
                                8009   800721
       Avedon, John F.
          An Interview with the Dalai Lama
            (Littlebird Publications)

Photographs Copyright © 1979 Richard Avedon
All rights reserved

ISBN 0-937896-00-4 paperback

Contents

ACKNOWLEDGEMENTS	7
PREFACE	9
I. RELIGIOUS VALUE AND HUMAN SOCIETY	13
II. HIS LIFE	17
III. TIBET: TODAY AND TOMORROW	27
IV. THE UNIVERSE: MIND AND MATTER	39
V. CYCLIC EXISTENCE AND SENTIENT BEINGS	51
VI. EMPTINESS: THE TWO TRUTHS	67
NOTES	77
BIBLIOGRAPHY	83

Acknowledgements

I would like to thank Jann Wenner, publisher of Rolling Stone Magazine, for making this interview possible. He had the foresight to encourage a story little known in the West, yet of immense intrinsic value. I would also like to thank the Dalai Lama's translators, the Ven. Tenzin Geyché, His Holiness' private secretary and Professor Jeffrey Hopkins of the University of Virginia. In particular, both Professor Hopkins and Khyongla Rato Rimpoché, President of the Tibet Center in New York City, were tremendously helpful in checking the text and contributing to the notes. Without their efforts, the degree of accuracy herein, would be considerably less. Lastly, for his friendship, patience and profound generosity, my thanks to His Holiness are unending.

**The Dalai Lama
New York City 10-15-79**

Preface

Tenzin Gyatso, the Fourteenth Dalai Lama of Tibet, was born in the small farming village of Takster in the province of Amdo on July 6, 1935. At the age of two, following a nation-wide search, he was discovered to be the reincarnation of his predecessor, the great Thirteenth Dalai Lama. As was perennially the case in locating a new Dalai Lama, miraculous signs had indicated the child's whereabouts.

Shortly after the Thirteenth Dalai Lama's death in December, 1933, curious cloud formations, pierced by rainbows, appeared repeatedly over the northeast end of Lhasa. A giant star-shaped fungus grew overnight on the northeast pillar of the room wherein the Dalai Lama's corpse lay. A few days later, the deceased ruler's head was found to have turned. No longer facing south—the traditional direction of auspiciousness—it clearly pointed to the northeast.

In the spring of 1935, the Regent of Tibet, accompanied by members of the National Assembly, journeyed to the sacred lake of Lhamoi Latso seeking a vision of the newborn Dalai Lama. Standing alone on a high rock, he peered into the water, believed by Tibetans to reflect the future. A great monastery, capped by jade and gold rooftops, floated into view. A narrow trail wound east from the monastery to a barren hilltop. Across from the hill, a house with turquoise tiles and a brown and white spotted dog was seen. Finally, three letters from the Tibetan alphabet came forth signifying, it was assumed, the specific town and province. Soon after this vision—which was set down in a secret report to the government—the Regent had a dream. Again he saw the same humble farmer's house. This time, however, there was a small boy in its courtyard, standing beneath oddly shaped gutter pipes emerging from the roof.

Guided by the vision, search parties fanned out across Tibet. One group traveled over a thousand miles northeast to Kum Bum Monastery, renowned for its jade and gold rooftops. From there, monks led them to a house with turquoise tiles set into its walls, located in the nearby village of Takster. Disguised as merchants, the party arrived at the door and requested to make tea in the kitchen, a common custom of Tibetan travelers.

On being admitted into the courtyard, the group's leader, Kyetsang Rimpoché of Sera Monastery, was struck by the building's oddly designed water spouts, made of gnarled juniper wood. He also noted the presence of a brown and white spotted dog. Dressed in an old sheepskin cloak, Rimpoché had chosen the role of servant to the party. Thus, while his own assistants were tended to by the man and woman of the house, he was free to look around.

As Kyetsang Rimpoché approached the kitchen, a little boy came running toward him, greatly excited. Sitting in his lap, the child grabbed a rosary that had belonged to the Thirteenth Dalai Lama but now hung around the visitor's neck. "I'll give it to you," said the monk "if you can guess who I am." "You are a lama of Sera," replied the boy correctly. He then went on to name the party's two other members—neither of whom he had even seen. Most remarkable of all, the child spoke in the refined dialect of Lhasa, unknown to almost anyone in his district.

Their interest greatly aroused, the party stayed the night, planning to leave unnoticed before dawn the next day. They weren't up early enough. The little boy had risen before them, and on seeing the troup prepare to depart, pleaded to be taken along. They succeeded in placating him only by promising to return. When they did, it was to submit him to a battery of tests in which articles of the past Dalai Lama were offered side by side with skillfully duplicated fakes. In each instance, the child chose the correct item, complaining bitterly as he did so, that it by rights, belonged to him. Further tests were pursued culminating in a physical inspection. Of the eight marks which distinguish the Dalai Lama from other men, the boy reportedly had every one. There was no longer any doubt. Here, just entering his second year of life, was the "Precious Protector" himself, the Fourteenth Dalai Lama of Tibet.

Tenzin Gyatso was brought to Lhasa at the age of four and a half. Within two weeks of his arrival, he was installed on the Lion Throne as the supreme temporal and spiritual ruler of Tibet. He spent his childhood in the company of monks and attendants with rare visits from his family. In the winter he lived in the Potala, the hilltop palace of the Dalai Lamas; during the summer, in the more informal gardens and pavilions of the Norbulinka or Jewel Park. He is reported by all who knew him to have been a self-confident and engaging child, one who took naturally to the role of Dalai Lama. As he grew older his curiousity concerning the world beyond Tibet led him into a round of self-assumed research, including the study of English, science, and mathematics. In his own Buddhist studies, he was recognized by his tutors to be unparalleled.

On October 7, 1950, Communist China invaded Tibet. Not yet sixteen, the Dalai Lama was forced to assume full temporal power despite his lack of experience in both government and international politics. For nine years, thereafter, he sought compromise with the Communists, believing that he alone could assuage the effect of their occupation upon his people. In March of 1959, however, a popular uprising against the Chinese (beginning three years earlier in the province of Kham) erupted in Lhasa itself. The Dalai Lama escaped to India, followed by over one hundred thousand refugees fleeing a brutal suppression; one which eventually was to claim more than half a million lives, and result in the almost complete destruction of the traditional Tibetan culture.

It has now been two decades since the Tibetan exiles arrived in India. During that time they have sought to preserve their culture as a means of struggling for Tibet's freedom. Resettled on over fifty large scale agricultural communities, they have, in effect, built an alternate Tibet abroad; one more truly Tibetan in character than that nation itself under China. Over the past year, their efforts have produced significant results. Recognizing that the Tibetan people continue to regard the Dalai Lama as their rightful leader, Peking has inaugurated an all-out attempt to woo the exiles home. To date, four delegations representing the Tibetan Government-in-exile have visited their homeland, reopening ties between friends and relatives that had been entirely severed until now. In addition, China has announced a set of major reforms in its colonial regime. Though the specific nature of a solution to the question of Tibet remains outstanding, it seems inevitable that a nation divided will shortly reunite.

In the midst of these abruptly altering circumstances, the Dalai Lama made his first visit to the United States. Arriving at Kennedy Airport on September 3, 1979, he undertook a twenty two city tour, during the course of which the following interview was conducted for Rolling Stone Magazine. It was produced in six sessions totalling eight hours: one in Charlottesville, Virginia; two in Los Angeles; and two at the Green Gulch Zen Farm, north of San Francisco. A final session was held in November of 1979 in Dharamsala, India, seat of the Tibetan Government-in-exile and His Holiness' residence since 1960. The interview proper is preceded by excerpts from a speech given at Constitution Hall in Washington, D.C. Offered in one form or another to audiences everywhere, the talk briefly summarizes the Dalai Lama's views on the human condition.

John Avedon
New York City
Summer, 1980

I.

Religious Value And Human Society

In this present generation, in a way, we have reached a high level of development. At the same time, we human beings are facing many problems. Certain problems are due to external or natural events. These we cannot avoid. Others are due to our own mental defects—something lacking inside. Because of them we have extra suffering. Now unless we have the right attitude in our minds towards society, towards mankind, material development alone is not sufficient. This is quite clear. If we adopt a right attitude, however, then these man-made problems might not occur.

The basic point is compassion; love for others, concern for their suffering, less selfishness. I feel compassionate thought is most precious. Only we human beings can develop it in our own hearts. If we have this—a good heart, a warm heart—we ourselves will be happy and satisfied. Our friends also will be. By that, nation to nation, country to country, continent to continent, perhaps, we can come to enjoy a friendly atmosphere and real peace.

The question is, how to develop compassion? Basically, this has to do with the feeling of "I". On a conventional level, there is an "I". "I want, I do not want"—one's own experience. With that feeling, we by nature want happiness and do not want suffering. In addition, we have the right to obtain happiness and to avoid suffering. Now, as I myself have this feeling and right, others also have the same. The difference is that when you say "I", it is just one single person whereas others are limitless. You can visualize this. On one side imagine your own "I", which so far has just concentrated on selfish motives. Put it close before you. Beyond it imagine others; limitless beings. Your present self becomes a third person looking on. You can see then that the feeling of wanting happiness and not wanting suffering is equal between the two: absolutely the same. The right to obtain happiness is also identical. No matter how renowned or wealthy the selfishly motivated person is, he or she is only one. No matter how poor the others are, they are infinite. Naturally, the many are more important than the one. So you see, if I use the infinite beings for myself, it is absolutely wrong—even if I can, I may not be happy. However, if I contribute or serve as much as I can, then that will be a source of great joy.

It is in terms of this attitude that you can develop real love for others. This type of compassionate development can even extend to your enemy. Our ordinary sense of love is very much related with attachment. With your own wife or husband, children or parents, you have some reason to love. Because it is "my" mother, "my" father, "my" children, I love them. This love is centered on a selfish motive. On the other hand is the clear recognition of the importance of others. If you develop compassion from this viewpoint, then that will reach your enemy. In order to generate such a motivation, we must have tolerance, patience. Without tolerance, it is difficult to develop this. Now who gives you this chance? Your enemy does. Your enemy can teach you tolerance. Your own teacher, your own parent cannot. So the enemy is actually very helpful for you. The enemy is really your best friend, your best teacher. If you can think that way, if you can cultivate this kind of attitude, then you will experience infinite compassion for all beings.

According to my own experience, the best feeling of gain comes from the most difficult period in one's life. If you go an easy way—everything is OK—then one day when you face certain problems, you'll feel depressed. However, it is mainly through difficulty that you learn. From it you gain inner strength, courage, determination. Now again, who gives you the chance for this? Your enemy does. It does not mean that you obey or bow down to him. Sometimes, according to the enemies' attitude, you may have to take strong action. It may be necessary to do so, but deep down without losing calmness and compassion. It is possible. Some people may feel or think "Now the Dalai Lama is talking nonsense," but this is not the case. If you practice, if you test this by your own experience; then you will see, you will feel it. OK?

I call this kind of love that I am describing, religion. This sort of compassion is the real essence of religion. On this level there is hardly any difference between Buddhism, Christianity or any other faith. All religions place emphasis on bettering human beings, on improving man. Brotherhood, love—these things are in common. Therefore, I always feel-as well as say to other Buddhists-that the question of nirvana will come later. There is not much hurry. But in day to day life, if you lead a good life, honest, compassionate, less selfish, then automatically it will lead to nirvana. In contrast, if you talk a lot about nirvana and do not bother much about day to day practice, then you will reach some strange enlightenment. You will not reach the correct one because in reality your daily practice is nothing. So you see, we must implement these good teachings in life. Whether you believe in God or not, it doesn't matter. Whether you believe in Buddha or not, it doesn't matter. You must lead a good life. Good food, good clothes, good shelter is not sufficient. A good motive is needed.

Now, in this present world atmosphere some people may think that religion is for those who remain in remote places: that it is not needed much in the business or political fields. My answer is no. All actions are founded in motivations, except certain minor ones. In politics, if you have a good motivation, then I think you will become an honest politician. Without such a motive what you do will be called dirty politics. In and of themselves, the politics are necessary to solve human problems—they are not bad—but when they are practiced by a selfish, a common person, then there is something lacking. Not only in politics, in religion as well. If I practice with a self-centered motive, then that religion becomes bad. So here you see, motivation is all important. Therefore, my simple practice is love, respect for others, honesty, teachings that cover the field of business, economy—everywhere.

At the present moment, if you look deeply at society, there are many problems. Deep down there is a feeling of unrest among almost everyone. Because of this feeling, it is not clear how to solve our problems. Now, I am not criticizing others, but you see, with real lasting peace inside, anger and hatred is impossible. On the other hand, wanting to benefit others, but deep down having a selfish motive, this also is impossible. We may talk a lot about peace, love, justice, but when certain things are related to us personally, we forget all of it. It is necessary to make war. It is necessary to suppress others, we say. When these things are heard, it is a clear sign of something lacking.

My feeling is simply this. If in this present atmosphere, in which everything depends on money and power, and there is not much concern about the real value of love, if we human beings now lose the value of justice, of compassion, of honesty, then in the future we will face more difficulty; more suffering will come. So it is hard, but absolutely worthwhile to try. If we try our best, whether we succeed or not is a different question. Even if we do not succeed in this life, alright, but at least we may attempt a better human society on the basis of love. So this is my feeling, this is my thinking on the relationship of religious value to human society.

II.

His Life

JA: What were your first feelings on being recognized as the Dalai Lama? What did you think had happened to you?

DL: I was very happy. I liked it a lot. Even before I was recognized, I often told my mother that I was going to go to Lhasa. I used to straddle a window sill in our house pretending that I was riding a horse to Lhasa. I was a very small child at the time, but I remember this clearly. I had a strong desire to go there. Another thing I didn't mention in my autobiography[1] is that after my birth, a pair of crows came to roost on the roof of our house. They would arrive each morning, stay for a while and then leave. This is of particular interest as similar incidents occurred at the birth of the First, Seventh, Eighth and Twelfth Dalai Lamas. After their births, a pair of crows came and remained. In my own case, in the beginning, nobody paid attention to this. Recently, however, perhaps three years ago, I was talking with my mother, and she recalled it. She had noticed them come in the morning, depart after a time, and then the next morning come again. Now, the evening after the birth of the First Dalai Lama, bandits broke into the family's house. The parents ran away and left the child. The next day when they returned and wondered what had happened to their son, they found the baby in a corner of the house. A crow stood before him, protecting him. Later on, when the First Dalai Lama grew up and developed in his spiritual practice, he made direct contact during meditation with the protective deity, Mahakala.[2] At this time, Mahakala said to him, "Somebody like you who is upholding the Buddhist teaching needs a protector like me. Right on the day of your birth, I helped you." So we can see, there is definitely a connection between Mahakala, the crows, and the Dalai Lamas.

There is another story related to this. The scholars of Nalanda,[3] the great Buddhist university, were once challenged to a debate by Ashvaghosha, a famous Hindu teacher. At that time, the tradition was that whoever lost a debate had to convert to the faith of the victor. Now Nalanda was the most important of the Buddhist universities. If it fell in debate, the teaching would be severely threatened. The scholars of Nalanda were so worried that they decided to send for Nagarjuna,[4] the greatest scholar of the time. Nagarjuna, however, was far away in southern India, too far for a man to take the note. Since they didn't have time, they decided to turn the matter over to Mahakala. They prayed and engaged in an elaborate and formal ceremony. Then they placed the letter they had written before the statue of Mahakala, whereupon Mahakala—through the statue—emanated a crow who took the letter and traveled to south India. On receiving it, Nagarjuna understood that Nalanda was in a desperate situation. He determined that his disciple, Aryadeva, would be the best one to debate Ashvaghosha. Therefore, he trained Aryadeva by engaging in intensive debate with him. At one point, Aryadeva got carried away and behaved in a slightly prideful manner with his teacher. Nagarjuna said this was alright, but because of it, a bad dependent-arising[5] would be created. Traveling back to Nalanda, Aryadeva was intercepted by a group of bandits and lost one of his eyes. Nevertheless, he arrived in Nalanda and successfully defeated Ashvaghosha. Ashvaghosha then became a student of Nagarjuna and wrote his books after that.

JA: Is the connection with the crow because it is black, like Mahakala, or is there something in the crow itself? Have crows appeared in your life since then?

DL: Actually, I don't like crows. Crows are generally very cruel to small birds. They always pester and bother them as well as attacking them. Another thing that happened, which my mother remembers very clearly, is that soon after I arrived in Lhasa, I said that my teeth were in a box in a certain house in the Norbulinka. When they opened the box, they found a set of dentures which had belonged to the Thirteenth Dalai Lama. I pointed to the box, and said that my teeth were in there, but right now I don't recall this at all. The new memories associated with this body are stronger. The past has become smaller, more vague. Unless I made a specific attempt to develop such a memory, I don't recall it.

JA: Do you remember your birth or the womb state before?

DL: At this moment, I don't remember. Also, I can't recall if at that time when I was a small child, I could remember it. However, there was one slight external sign perhaps. Children are usually born with their eyes closed. I was born with my eyes open. This may be some slight indication of a clear state of mind in the womb.

JA: When you were a little boy, how did you feel on being treated by adults as an important person? Were you apprehensive or even frightened at being so revered?

DL: Tibetans are very practical people. Older Tibetans would never treat me that way. Also, I was very self-confident. When I first approached Lhasa on the Debuthang plain, the Nechung Oracle came to further verify that I was the correct choice. With him came an old, very respected, and highly realized geshay[6] from Loseling College of Drepung Monastery.[7] He was deeply concerned whether or not I was the correct choice. To have made a mistake in finding the Dalai Lama would be very dangerous. Now he was a religious man—not someone in the government. He came into the tent where I was in a group audience, and determined that unquestionably I was the right choice. So you see, though there were certain very proper old people who wanted to be sure, I apparently put on a good performance and convinced them (laughter). I was never uneasy in my position. Charles Bell[8] has mentioned that I was taking it all quite casually. To do with fear, there's one thing I remember clearly. One night I wanted to go visit my mother, who had come with the rest of my family to Lhasa. I was in the tent of the Regent. A very large bodyguard was standing by the entrance. It was evening, sunset, and this man had a bad, damaged eye. I remember being scared, frightened then, to go out of the tent. So, like that. There are many mysterious things, stories, when you talk about rebirth.

JA: Perhaps you could describe your feelings for your teachers. They seem to have played a major role in your upbringing.

DL: Nothing in particular. When I first met Ling Rimpoché[9] as a small boy, I was a little afraid. When I got older, the fear gradually disappeared, and respect replaced it. So like that, not much.

JA: Between the ages of sixteen and eighteen, after you assumed temporal power, did you change?

DL: Yes, I changed . . . a little bit. I underwent a lot of happiness and pain. Within that and from growing, gaining more experience, from the problems that arose and the suffering, I changed. The ultimate result is the man you see now (laughter).

JA: How about when you just entered adolescence? Many people have a difficult time defining themselves as an adult. Did this happen to you?

DL: No. My life was very much in a routine. Two times a day I studied. Each time I studied for an hour, and then spent the rest of the time playing (laughter). Then at the age of 13, I began studying philosophy, definitions, debate. My study increased, and I also studied caligraphy. It was all in a routine though, and I got used to it. Sometimes, there were vacations. These were very comfortable; happy. Losang Samten, my immediate elder brother, was usually at school, but during these times he would come to visit. Also, occasionally my mother would bring special bread from our province of Amdo. Very thick and delicious. She made this herself.

JA: Did you have an opportunity to have a relationship with your father when you were growing up?

DL: My father died when I was 13. This is in my book.

JA: Are there any of your predecessors with whom you have a particular affinity or interest in?

DL: The Thirteenth Dalai Lama. He brought a lot of improvement to the standards of study in the monastic colleges. He gave great encouragement to the real scholars. He made it impossible for people to go up in the religious hierarchy, becoming an abbot and so forth, without being totally qualified. He was very strict in this respect. He also gave tens of thousands of monks ordinations. These were his two main religious achievements. He didn't give many initiations, or many lectures. Now, with respect to the country, he had great thought and consideration for statescraft—the outlying districts in particular—how they should be governed and so forth. He cared very much about how to run the government more efficiently. He had great concern about our borders and that type of thing.

JA: During the course of your own life, what have been your greatest personal lessons or internal challenges? Which realizations and experiences have had the most effect on your growth as an individual?

DL: Regarding religious experience, some understanding of shunya[10]—some feeling, some experience—and mostly bodhichitta,[11] altruism. It has helped a lot. In some ways, you could say that it has made me into a new person, a new man. I'm still progressing. Trying. It gives you inner strength, courage, and it is easier to accept situations. That's one of the greatest experiences.

JA: *On the bodhichitta side, are you speaking about a progressive deepening of realization or a certain moment associated with external experience?*

DL: Mainly internal practice. There could also be external causes or circumstances. External factors could have played a part in the development of some feeling for bodhichitta. But mainly, it has to come from internal practice.

JA: *Can you cite a specific moment from your practice when you crossed a threshold?*

DL: Regarding shunya theory, first shunya theory, then bodhichitta feeling . . . Around '65, '66, in that period. This is really a personal matter. For a true religious practitioner, these things must be kept private.

JA: *OK. Not asking you about your own deepest experience, but in terms of the course of your life—the events of your life—how have these affected you as a man? How have you grown through experiencing them?*

DL: Being a refugee has been very useful. You are much closer to reality. When I was in Tibet as the Dalai Lama, I was trying to be realistic, but somehow because of circumstances, there was some distance, I think. I was a bit isolated from the reality. I became a refugee. Very good. So there was a good opportunity to gain experience, and also determination or inner strength.

JA: *When you became a refugee, what helped you gain this strength? Was it the loss of your position and country, the fact of everyone suffering around you? Were you called on to lead your people in a different way than you had been accustomed to?*

DL: Being a refugee is a really desperate, dangerous situation. At that time, everyone deals with reality. It is not the time to pretend things are beautiful. That's something. You feel involved with reality. In peace time, everything goes smoothly. Even if there is a problem, people pretend that things are good. They can practice that during a peaceful or smooth time. During a dangerous period, when there's a dramatic change, then there's no scope to pretend that everything is fine. You must accept that bad is bad. Now when I left the Norbulinka, there was danger. We were passing very near the Chinese military barracks. It was just on the other side of the river, the Chinese checkpost there. You see, we had definite information two or three weeks before I left, that the Chinese were fully prepared to attack us. It was only a question of the day and hour.

JA: At that moment, when you crossed the Kyichu river and met the party of Khamba guerillas waiting for you, did you assume a direct leadership capacity? Who, for instance, made the decisions on your flight?

DL: As soon as we left Lhasa, we set up an inner group, a committee to discuss each point. Myself and eight other people.

JA: Was it your idea to make it unanimous?

DL: Yes. Those who were left behind in Lhasa also established a People's Committee. Something like a revolutionary council. Of course, from the Chinese viewpoint, this was a counter revolutionary committee. Chosen by the people, you see, within a few days . . . They set up that committee and all major decisions were made by it. I also sent a letter to that committee, certifying it. In our small committee, those who were escaping with me, we discussed the practical points each night. We would sit together, and discuss, but not always. Originally, our plan was to establish our headquarters in southern Tibet, as you know. In my book, I discussed these things. Also, I mentioned to Pandit Nehru—I think on the 24th of April, 1959—that we had established a Tibetan temporary government, shifted from Lhasa to southern Tibet. I mentioned this casually to the Prime Minister. He was slightly agitated (laughter). "We are not going to recognize your government," he said. Although this government had been formed while still inside Tibet, and I was already in India . . .

JA: I'd like to ask you about being the incarnation of the Bodhisattva of Infinite Compassion, Avalokiteshvara. How do you personally feel about this? Is it something you have an unequivocal view of one way or another?

DL: It is difficult for me to say definitely. Unless I engaged in a meditative effort, such as following my life back breath by breath, I couldn't say exactly. We believe that there are four types of rebirth. One, which is the common type, wherein a being is helpless to determine his or her rebirth, but only incarnates in dependence on the nature of past actions. The opposite is that of an entirely enlightened Buddha, who simply manifests a physical form to help others. In this case, it is clear that the person is a Buddha. A third is one who due to past spiritual attainment, can choose, or at least influence, the place and situation of rebirth. The fourth is called a blessed manifestation. In this the person is blessed beyond his normal capacity to perform helpful functions, such as teaching religion. For this last type of birth, the person's wishes in previous lives to help others must have been very strong. They then obtain such empowerment. Though some seem more likely than others, I cannot definitely say which I am.

JA: From the viewpoint then of the realistic role you play as Chenrezi, how do you feel about it? Only a few people in history have been considered, in one way or another, divine. Is the role a burden or a delight?

DL: It is very helpful. Through this role I can be of great benefit to people. For this reason I like it; I'm at home with it. It's clear that it is very helpful to people, and that I have the karmic relationship to be in this role. Also, it is clear that there is a karmic relationship with the Tibetan people in particular. Now you see, you may consider that under the circumstances, I am very lucky. However, behind the word luck, there are actual causes or reasons. There is the karmic force of my ability to assume this role as well as the force of my wish to do so. In regard to this, there is a statement in the great Shantideva's *Engaging in the Bodhisattva Deeds* which says, "As long as space exists, and as long as there are migrators in cyclic existence, may I remain—removing their suffering." I have that wish in this lifetime, and I know I had that wish in past lifetimes.

JA: With such a vast goal as your motivation, how do you deal with your personal limitations, your limits as a man?

DL: Again, as it says in Shantideva, "If the blessed Buddha cannot please all sentient beings, then how could I?" Even an enlightened being, with limitless knowledge and power and the wish to save all others from suffering, cannot eliminate the individual karma of each being.

JA: Is this what keeps you from being overwhelmed when you see the suffering of the six million Tibetans, who on one level, you are responsible for?

DL: My motivation is directed towards all sentient beings. There is no question, though, that on a second level, I am directed towards helping Tibetans. If a problem is fixable, if a situation is such that you can do something about it, then there is no need to worry. If it's not fixable, then there is no help in worrying. There is no benefit in worrying whatsoever.

JA: A lot of people say this, but few really live by it. Did you always feel this way, or did you have to learn it?

DL: It is developed from inner practice. From a broader perspective, there will always be suffering. On one level, you are bound to meet with the effects of the unfavorable actions you yourself have previously committed in either body, speech or mind. Then also, your very own nature is that of suffering. There's not just one factor figuring into my attitude, but many different ones. From the point of view of the actual entity producing the suffering, as I have said, if it is fixable, then there is no need to worry. If not, there is no benefit to worry. From the point of view of the cause, suffering is based on past unfavorable actions accumulated by oneself and no other. These karmas are not wasted. They will bear their fruit. One will not meet with the effects of actions that one has not done oneself. Finally, from the viewpoint of the nature of suffering itself, the aggregates of the mind and body have as their actual nature, suffering. They serve as a basis for suffering. As long as you have them you are susceptible to suffering. From a deep point of view, while we don't have our independence and are living in someone else's country, we have a certain type of suffering, but when we return to Tibet and gain our independence, then there will be other types of suffering. So, this is just the way it is. You might think that I'm pessimistic, but I am not. This is the Buddhist realism. This is how, through Buddhist teaching and advice, we handle situations. When fifty-thousand people in the Shakya clan were killed one day, Shakyamuni Buddha, their clansman, didn't suffer at all. He was leaning against a tree, and he was saying, "I am a little sad today because fifty-thousand of my clansmen were killed." But he, himself, remained unaffected. Like that, you see (laughter). This was the cause and effect of their own karma. There was nothing he could do about it. These sorts of thoughts make me stronger; more active. It is not at all a case of losing one's strength of mind or will in the face of the pervasive nature of suffering.

JA: When you experience happy feelings, how do you stay detached from them?

DL: From the point of giving up one's household or home, as a monk does, many limits are set on your life and behavior. These automatically give one contentment. It depends on your attitude. If you have a disposition which wants more, then when you go into a store, you'll want everything there or even everything in all stores. But if your attitude is to want just what is needed, then none of it is needed.

JA: I'm interested in what you do to relax: gardening and experimenting with electronics.

DL: Oh, my hobbies. Passing time (laughter). When I can repair something, it gives me real satisfaction. I began dismantling things when I was young because I was curious about how certain machines functioned. I wanted to know what was inside the motor, but these days I only try to fix something when it breaks.

JA: And gardening?

DL: Gardening in Dharamsala is almost a hopeless thing. No matter how hard you work, the monsoon comes and destroys everything. You know, a monk's life is very gratifying; very happy. You can see this from those who have given up the robes. They definitely know the value of monkhood. Many have told me how complicated and difficult life is without it. With a pretty wife and children you might be happy for some time. In the long run, though, many problems naturally come about. Half of your independence—your freedom—is lost. If there is some benefit or meaning to experiencing the trouble which arises on giving up your independence, then it is worthwhile. If it is an effective situation which helps people, then it is good. The trouble becomes worthwhile. But if it isn't, it is not worthwhile.

JA: But none of us would even be here talking about this unless we had mothers and fathers!

DL: I'm not saying that having children is bad, or that everyone should be a monk. Impossible (laughter). I think that if one's life is simple, contentment has to come. Simplicity is extremely important for happiness. Having few desires, feeling satisfied with what you have is very vital. There are four causes which help produce a superior being. Satisfaction with whatever food you get. Satisfaction with rags for clothing, or acceptance of any covering—not wishing for fancy or colorful attire. Satisfaction with just enough shelter to protect yourself from the elements. And finally, an intense delight in abandoning faulty states of mind and in cultivating helpful ones in meditation.

III.

Tibet: Today And Tomorrow

JA: Could you describe current conditions in Tibet, as far as you are aware of them?

DL: Each day the labor period is ten or twelve hours, sometimes fourteen. Therefore, the Tibetans say there are only three things to see. In the morning you see the stars, during the day the locks on the houses, and at night, returning from work, the moon. After work they must remain another two or three hours at political meetings, accusing one another and engaging in so-called class-struggle—forced by the Chinese to create problems. From school going age to the age of seventy, eighty, ninety, people must work. Recently, a Tibetan from Dharamsala secretly went to his native home in western Tibet. According to him, when he came to visit his own mother who was about seventy, she had no time to see him. "Why don't you take a few days off so that we can be together?," he asked. His mother replied that she couldn't because she would lose work points. Without points, she would not eat. Where his mother was working, he also saw people in their eighties and nineties working. This is so the Chinese can take grain for many different purposes.

JA: In terms of the overall environment, how much restriction is there on freedom of speech?

DL: To speak out in public is very difficult. Though there is some leniency nowadays, many Tibetans feel that this recent liberalization is another trick, like the One Hundred Thousand Flowers Movement. At that time, everywhere, including Tibet, the Chinese government encouraged people to express their own thoughts. Actually, this was just a means on the part of the government to discover who the so-called "main reactionaries" were. During the short period it lasted, they marked down the name of everyone who spoke up. Then the movement concluded, and under the name of another popular movement or policy, they gathered up all the people they had identified. That is their practice. So you see, freedom of speech is very strict; limited. Recently, there have been quite a number of posters put up in Lhasa. The extent of liberalization that is now taking place in China, though, has not come to Tibet.

JA: Is the country very much an armed camp? After 30 years, is it still occupied by Chinese troops?

DL: Practically wherever there is a Tibetan population, there also is a big Chinese military camp. In the border area, it is understandable to have large military camps, but inside, if things were quite normal, then why would it be necessary to station large numbers of soldiers everywhere? In Lhasa alone, the Han military and civilian population is more than the Tibetan population.

JA: Is there a large prison system? Are there many political prisoners?

DL: Yes. Near Lhasa, northeast of the city, there is one large prison camp which right now has at least two thousand fresh prisoners. They come from a remote part of Tibet and were arrested as a result of having taken part in a revolt, an uprising. Most of these prisoners are young people. According to one very recent source of information, the torture and hardship being carried out on the Tibetans in that camp is so great that the people who have told us this find it difficult to explain. It is too upsetting. This is just one camp. In other places there are still prisoners.

JA: What is your knowledge of the Tibetan underground? Is it constituted in separate movements?

DL: Among the youth, the underground and nationalistic feeling is quite strong. It is really remarkable. It seems that there are organizations; but in terms of numbers and this sort of thing, it is hard to say, and also there is not much value to do so. Actual physical resistance, fighting, is quite rare. It is too difficult. As I mentioned, the Chinese fully control the country. However, they are always moving about in groups or convoys because of the danger of Tibetans attacking them. Occasionally, there is sabotage.

Now I will tell you about food. Animal husbandry has greatly increased as well as food production, but any real benefit for our people is very limited. In the last year or two, the food conditions around Lhasa have become a little better, but around the countryside, it is very poor. During the past eighteen years or so the people were half hungry all the time.

JA: Has that increased disease and infant mortality?

DL: Oh, yes. Many people, just because they couldn't get any butter—a staple of their diet from childhood—developed serious stomach ailments. They would swell up with gas. Their faces would become bloated, and many died. People are forced to eat just whatever wild vegetables they can find. Also, as I mentioned, the Chinese take increasing amounts of grain under different excuses or names. They say, "For love of your government, you must contribute more grain to it." That is one tax. Another one requires that more grain be sold to the government. The fee which the people are supposed to receive in payment is to be collected at the bank, but usually they never get this money. Then the Chinese take grain to prepare for the Third World War. In the past, they said this was inevitable due to American imperialism, now it is supposed to come as a result of Soviet revisionism. In any case, according to the Chinese, there will be a Third World War. So they tell Tibetans that preparation for this war is highly necessary and then they take another portion of grain. As a result of all this, the quantity of grain that should last thirty days lasts only twenty. Generally, Tibetans have quite big stomachs. They are used to eating well. If the people really ate to fill their stomachs, the grain wouldn't last more than twenty or twenty-five days. In order to make up for the lack of rations, they often brew a very light soup to stretch it to the end of the month. In one way they are developing good eating habits. They certainly won't get fat (laughter).

Now another point. Tibetans drink tea which is thickly brewed with butter, but the ration of butter given out is very small, completely insufficient to make ordinary butter tea. Therefore, they put a tiny portion of butter, a pinch, in the cup. Also, as you might know, Tibetans are big meat eaters. We are very fond of it. In the past, meat was always available. Now, they can only get meat on Tibetan New Years and the first of October, the anniversary of the founding of the People's Republic. So, on only two or three occasions a year do they get meat. In some places, like Kham,[12] it is even worse. One man from that area, who usually lives in Peking, had one of his children visit his birthplace. According to what he said to someone, who in turn told me, that place had plenty of meat in the past. Now, the father is a Communist, a Tibetan Communist. The son stayed there one year. During the entire year he didn't see one piece of meat. This is the son of a party member. The father had already joined the Chinese Communist Party in the early thirties. Until 1957 he was one of the main Tibetan Communists who were working with the Chinese. This person is one of my best friends. In 1954-55, when I was in Peking, most of the time I met Mao Zedong and other Chinese dignitaries, this person was my interpreter. I trusted him. Though he was a Communist, he was a patriotic Tibetan. He was supposed to remain in Tibet permanently, but one day he came to see me. He told me that he had received a telegram from Peking saying that he was to immediately return there. After some time the main Chinese representative stationed in Tibet, told me at a meeting that this person was a very bad element; nasty, narrow and nationalistic. He committed many crimes—such as trying to establish a Tibetan Communist Party. "Now he will never come back," he said. So he disappeared in '57. For the past twenty-three years, I have been worried about him. Just a short time ago, though, I was told that he is in Peking. That is his story.

Now education. In central Tibet, two or three years back, we heard on Radio Lhasa propaganda that there were more than three thousand primary schools and a few middle schools. Recently, the Chinese said that there are six thousand primary schools in central Tibet. No doubt there are several thousand. The real standard of education, though, is very, very low. This is obvious. In China, itself, the standard of education is not very high. In the past two or three decades there has been more emphasis on ideaology than education. So you see, with minorities like the Tibetans, there is no question that the standard of education is low. Furthermore, the Chinese place major emphasis on learning Chinese rather than Tibetan. Tibetan is taught, but primarily Chinese. The period of real study is very brief. Mainly the children are forced to labor, killing mosquitoes and rats. They are sent out after just a short study period, and the rest of the time they are used as workers. The food conditions for school boys and girls are also bad. In many cases, particularly in rural areas, they are made to bring their food from home where it is very scarce. Now in Lhasa, in a certain middle school, there are Chinese children. This is the type of place where it is supposed to be better, but here the food for Tibetan and Chinese children is separate. There are two categories: one is called bread eaters, the other, rice eaters. The Chinese belong to the rice eaters kitchen, the Tibetans to the other. The quality of the food of the rice eaters is very good, certainly better than that of the bread eaters. In the morning, the Chinese children get hot water to wash their faces with, the Tibetans, cold. This I have heard directly from a teacher who taught in that school for three years and escaped to India. She told me this story. Among the teachers, again the Tibetans get less pay, the Chinese, more. Near Lhasa—in a school east of it—the Tibetan students have been getting stale or rotten food for the past few years. Due to that food, most of the students got very sick. Many of them have said that they never want to be born again in such a place. Also, during the Cultural Revolution, the Chinese attempted to restructure all of Tibetan grammar. They made some really stupid changes. Most often, what they wrote is absolutely unintelligible.

Now health. There are many clinics. There are also the famous barefoot doctors. One good thing is that the Chinese respect traditional Tibetan medicine. They have actually built factories to make Tibetan medicine—one near Shigatse, one in the Khombo area in southeastern Tibet by the Indian border. They have also pursued some serious research in Tibetan medicine. This is very good, but the actual health conditions among the masses are different. The real benefit they get from these health centers is very little. Not much. There are clear indications of this. For instance, when someone enters a hospital, they are told that they need a blood test. Under the name of a blood test the Chinese take one, two, three large bottles of blood. Once the person leaves the clinic, he or she gets no medication or treatment. Perhaps one day they are free not to work and on some occasions, they will get a single egg. This is the situation. A group of foreign journalists visited Tibet recently, and noticed how poor the health of the children in Lhasa is. Lhasa is supposed to be the best place in the whole country.

Communications. There are many good roads, a few airfields, some buses, some Russian-made jeeps and some Japanese Toyotas; but mostly these are used by Chinese civilian and military officials—or certain Tibetans who are authorized to use them. The people—our people—are still walking wherever they have to go, using their legs. Perhaps because the roads are better now, there is less wear on their shoes (laughter). There are serious restrictions, as well. There is no question that one cannot go from village to village. Lhasa, itself, is divided into four sections. Without permission, a person in the southern section cannot go to the northern part. Now recently this sort of restriction has slightly eased. It seems a little change is occurring. Still, we are not at all satisfied. Also you might know that they have just changed the head of the so-called Tibetan Autonomous Region, the leader. The new person is a Tibetan, which the Chinese make a big point of for propaganda purposes. This person is called Tembo by the Chinese; in Tibetan, Sangay Yeshay. His choice is supposed to show the world that the leadership is in the hands of the Tibetans. Actually, I knew this person very well. He is a very good man, a very nice man, but unfortunately, when we spoke we needed an interpreter. He didn't speak Tibetan. When he was a very small boy, he was taken by the Red Army during their Long March. He was from then on completely cut off from any contact with Tibetans. His wife is Chinese. He spent his entire life in the Red Army. Personally, he is very nice, very simple, kind-hearted, humble. When you speak Tibetan to him, he would even feel embarrassed, and blush.

JA: Perhaps we can talk a bit about the situation in India. Since coming into exile, you've made a concerted effort to establish a more representative, democratic form of government than in the past—one almost feels as a self-conscious alternative to the Chinese rule of Tibet. What do you feel is the correct balance between majority decision and your particular right as Dalai Lama to choose what is best for your people?

DL: They work together. Though there are some complaints, some criticism, it is alright. Criticism is a healthy sign. Without it, like the Chinese—in the mouth, no criticism, but in the heart, criticism—it is no good. Open, outspoken criticism is very good. Generally, in the past twenty years, we have managed quite well. There are deputies who are elected by the people. The final approval of them is mine. The People's Deputies, who are elected in exile, only have authority from those in exile. The Dalai Lama, however, is someone who can represent all six million Tibetans. So you see, my approval of them is beneficial. It gives weight or authority to them. Also, the overall situation is that it is not our own country we are living in. It is a very, very peculiar circumstance. Under these conditions we must take every precaution. Now in most cases, if there are several candidates, I approve those who have had the highest votes. Suppose, however, there is a person who I feel cannot correctly handle the responsibility. I then have the authority to choose someone else. So far, I think this system has worked very well. It, itself, has gone through several changes. Now, besides the actual participation of the People's Deputies in the work of governing, the process of electing them—voting itself—is training for our people. How to select; how to vote. Sometimes they become very confused (laughter). This is important though. In the future we must go this way. In some cases, because this is new to the Tibetans, they mark the wrong name; they don't know who to choose (laughter), and so on, but it is very important to learn.

JA: What would you imagine as the ideal type of government for Tibet in the future?

DL: That is difficult to say. At least in India we have prepared some sort of situation for the future of Tibet according to our own draft constitution. We practice according to that as much as we can in a foreign land. In the future, from our side, we will be making some kind of presentation to our people inside. Now you see, we will discuss it, but the ultimate decision will be made by the Tibetans who are inside and have been for the last twenty years—whenever that time comes. Those people have really suffered. At least we are quite free, but they have really suffered. All credit goes to them. Because of their determination, we are inspired to work. For various reasons, the ultimate decision lies in their hands, not mine. Whatever governmental and economic system we will adopt will be entirely up to them. The Tibetan people, the younger Tibetans in particular, have gone through tremendous difficulties and have gained good experience. I am quite sure they will take the right path.

JA: I know it is hard to say at this point, but under what conditions would you go back to Tibet?

DL: My general explanation—our general aim—is that the people be happy. Now that is the main point. In detail, I don't want to say at the moment—and it is difficult to say. At the moment there is no question of returning. First, things must change inside; then, we'll see.

JA: By happiness of the people, what do you mean specifically?

DL: For the last thirty years, irrespective of the difference in classes, whether people are rich or poor, old or young, the majority have not been happy or satisfied. So first, this must be changed. So it is quite difficult . . .

JA: Can you define the difference between an autonomous Tibet and an independent Tibet?

DL: I'll just repeat that the main objective is the happiness of our people, the maximum benefit for our people. Besides that, I'm not going to say any particular word. More time should pass, then we will see.

JA: Why at this particular time, after 21 years of virtually no official contact, has a delegation representing the Tibetan Government-in-exile gone to visit Tibet?

DL: Because of the Chinese attitude. Their overall attitude has changed so we took this opportunity to send a delegation for our own people to look.

JA: Some Tibetans still speak in terms of taking their country back by force. Is there any way within your own personal beliefs that violence and religious views can work together? Or is it impossible?

DL: They can be combined. It depends on the motivation and the result. With a good motivation and result, and if under the circumstances there is no other alternative, then violence is permissible.

JA: Can you elaborate?

DL: A good motive means doing it for the benefit of the majority of the people. But now, here you see, regarding the Tibetan question, a military movement would be suicidal.

JA: Because of the overwhelming strength of the Chinese?

DL: Oh, yes.

JA: So you would discourage anyone who felt that this was a viable alternative?

DL: Sometimes a militant attitude or idea is helpful to maintain morale. In certain ways this idea is helpful, but I don't think it is feasible to actually take part in a military movement.

JA: Now that you have been through America, do you see any scope for speaking out more publically than in the past?

DL: I don't know. I haven't given any thought to it. These days, I've intensified studying my own Buddhist philosophy . . . not world politics (laughter). Naturally, as a result of my visit, more Americans will be interested in the Tibetan affair. Perhaps the papers in America might take up the Tibetan issue a little more. The more people who know the true situation in Tibet, the more difficult it will be for the Chinese to ignore the awareness of the world's people. Although there may not be any immediate or direct result, it will have this benefit in the long run.

JA: Speaking of world opinion, I've heard many people express a desire for you as a religious leader to contribute a spiritual perspective to the global situation. If you felt that people could benefit, would you pursue it?

DL: If it's going to be of any benefit, certainly—most definitely. I would be willing to contribute as much as I can. I have had this intention for many years as a Buddhist monk. It's not something special, particularly for someone who practices bodhichitta—altruism, compassion. Naturally, that feeling is there. In the future, also, anything I can contribute to the whole of mankind, as a human being, as a person who practices these things as a duty, a responsibility, of course I would.

JA: Other people have asked why you have been so isolated. Why is this the first time they are hearing from you? They wonder why you haven't been in the news more often.

DL: I had been speaking on these lines, but not many people were taking interest. When I went to Europe in 1973, the theme was the same, but there was more interest in the United States this time.

JA: Returning to the question of Tibet, can you say what the rela-

tionship of religion and government will be in the future? Is this something you have given thought to?

DL: This is complicated. When we say religion, the moral principle which is the essence of any religion, covers every field, including politics. I always say that the politician must have moral principles. So from that viewpoint, religion and politics go together. Without religion, politics might become something upon which nobody can rely, full of cunning and lies. If we are speaking about a religious institution, though, such as the church, then I think it should be seperate. I discussed this at Harvard. Now about this. In the United States Government, the state and church are separate—secular—yet when the President takes the oath of office, he holds the Bible and says the name of God. That shows that the head of state must be honest. When he takes the oath to carry out his duties in the office as truthfully and honestly as he can with God as his witness, this shows the moral principle in politics. If you mix an organized church with the state, however, there will be complications. Now here, about the Dalai Lama. When I am in my own home, then whatever practice I want to do or whatever tradition I want to follow is in my own hands. When I come to my office, then I myself believe and act as though I belong to no particular sect, or tradition. This shows that there is some kind of a separation—although externally, some people might think that the two things function together, are combined. For example, the Fifth Dalai Lama, before he took temporal power, belonged to one monastery. Once he took the responsibility as head of state, then he acted as someone who belonged to the entire religion, not just one particular group.

JA: In essence, you feel that you have the ability to separate these functions within your own person, yet, externally they seem to be embodied in one man. So it depends upon your own determination.

DL: It's something like Cyprus and Makarios. It's just a religious person being head of the government.

JA: Can you foresee in the future if religious officials will mirror lay officials the way they used to in the old Tibetan government?

DL: No. But it's possible. In the past, although occasionally there were lay people heading the government or the nation, generally, the people preferred a lama; but I feel that system might not continue in the future. It would be stupid just because of religious stubborness to say that we must have a lama. In the future, we will have to act according to what is necessary in the existing circumstances; what is most beneficial. Anyway, the future is very big, very open; anything is possible. It is very important to make a detailed and precise plan. At the same time, nobody knows what will happen, only time can answer that. The best thing is to act according to the situation itself, as it exists at that time. On the one hand, it's important to have a detailed plan of what you want to do. And at the same time you have to be flexible enough to act according to existing circumstances.

IV.

The Universe: Mind And Matter

JA: At what stage do you see mankind's evolution? For instance, if you were to look at the entire human race as one person, would you say we're in childhood, adolescence, adulthood?

DL: According to the general Buddhist teaching—Buddhist scriptures—sometimes the world is better, sometimes worse. Now if you speak about the period of one aeon, then our era is still childhood, but within a smaller period, it is old. I will explain. According to the Abhidharmakosha,[13] one great aeon is composed of eighty intermediate aeons in four groups of twenty. The first twenty are aeons of vacuity. The vacuity is the absence of the last world system. They are followed by twenty aeons of formation of the new world system; then twenty aeons of abiding; then twenty aeons of destruction of that system. Right now we're in the aeons of abiding. Within these twenty intermediate aeons of abiding, we are in the first long period of decline. So, as this one is coming down, there are eighteen ups and downs afterwards. Then the twentieth goes on up. Now we are in the first downward one, at the point in which the average lifespan is around a hundred years. In terms of this first period of decline, we are far along in it, and thus, old, but in terms of the twenty aeons of abiding, we are only at the beginning.

JA: Is this panoramic view from scriptural sources only?

DL: Yes.

JA: Is that the only proof that can be cited for this picture of time and space?

DL: I think so; probably just scriptural. But forget about all these aeons, it's even difficult for us to explain in terms of science the nearest star. Quite difficult.

JA: Where it is, or what it's like?

DL: What is its real cause, and so forth. What I'm talking about is one world system within a billion worlds, like explaining one galaxy.

JA: OK, let's go right to the beginning then. What is the Buddhist view of the origin of the universe?

DL: In terms of matter, it's really energy. In terms of the internal beings, or persons, the force that produces them is that of the actions they have accumulated, which cause them to be reborn in that way.

JA: Dealing first with the matter side of it, inanimate matter. What is the energy by which phenomena manifest?

DL: In terms of the elements, wind is first. Its basis is space. Then the wind moves, and in dependence on that, heat occurs; then moisture, then solidity—the earth element. If you have to explain what the initial wind is a continuation of, then probably it comes out of the period of vacuity of the former world system. In any case, it's infinite. If you speak about one world within a world system of a billion worlds, then you can speak about a beginning; otherwise, in general, you can't.

JA: But what is the direct cause, initially, of space; and secondly, of this wind or energy[14] you are speaking about.

DL: If you're speaking externally, then just what I said; the period of vacuity of the former world system.

JA: Energy spontaneously arises from vacuity?

DL: It's natural, not something fabricated, but behind that is karmic force.

JA: What is this karmic force?

DL: Of course, it's necessary to explain karma. Karma means action. For instance, I'm speaking now, and that's a verbal act. I'm moving my hands, and that's a physical act. Then there are mental actions which are cases in which there isn't any physical or verbal manifestation. Due to these actions, there are both immediate and long-range results. Because of our speaking, a certain atmosphere is generated here and that's an immediate effect. However, our speaking also establishes a potency, or makes an imprint on the continuum of the mind. Through this imprint there come to be further good, bad and neutral actions long after the original ones stop. Thus there are good, bad and neutral karmas. There is this state of destruction—the state of the activity's having ceased—and this remains in the mental continuum. This state of cessation is an affirming negative—an absence which includes something positive. It is a potency which is not just the mere cessation of the action, but has the capacity of producing an effect in the future. These states of cessation are capable of regenerating moment by moment until an effect is produced. When it meets with the proper conditions, it fructifies, or matures. It doesn't make any difference how much time passes. It could even be billions of aeons. If one hasn't engaged in a means to cause the potency to be reduced—such as confession and intention of restraint in the case of bad actions—then it will just remain.

JA: Where does it remain?

DL: With the continuum of the mind. There are two bases that are explained for this imprint. One is continual, the other temporary. The temporary one is the mental continuum, and the continual one is the mere "I", the relative self of a person.

JA: Not getting into such detail yet, but going all the way back to the beginning, what is the most basic difference between mind and matter?

DL: Matter is physical; mind is mere illumination and knowing.

JA: What has caused this mind?

DL: As regarding the causes of mind, there is a substantial cause, as well as cooperative conditions—an empowering condition and an observed object condition. This last condition—the object which is perceived—could be a form; but a form, a physical thing, cannot be the substantial cause of a mind. It must be something that, itself, is illuminating and knowing. For instance, when I look at the tape recorder, my eye consciousness has as its observed object condition the tape recorder. Its empowering condition—that which enables it to see color and shape—is the sense power of the eye, but its substantial cause (also called its preceeding condition), which generates it into an entity that is illuminating and knowing, must be a previous moment of illumination and knowing, a previous moment of consciousness.

JA: That entity which is illuminating and knowing: what has caused that? Is that spontaneous, too? Where does that originally come from?

DL: And thus there's no beginning to the mind.

JA: There is no beginning to the mind . . .

DL: No ending, either. With regard to specific minds and consciousnesses, there are beginnings and ends, but with regard to this mere factor of illumination and knowing, there's no beginning or end. Now, with some consciousnesses, there are cases where there is no beginning, but there is an end. For instance, an afflictive emotion. When you finally remove a specific mental affliction such as jealousy, then the continuum of that consciousness meets its end. The very nature of mind is that it is this thing which is illuminating and knowing. Right? There isn't anything further.

JA: That satisfies you to say it's just nature?

DL: There are four types of investigation of phenomena. One is by way of dependence, such as seeing that smoke depends on fire. Another is to notice the functions of things. The third is by way of reasoning; proving correctness or incorrectness. The last is the recognition that such and such is the object's nature. For instance, that we want happiness is just our nature. There's nothing else to discover. Now, with regard to universal causation, either you have to accept a creative deity, or you have to accept that the universe is beginningless. There's no other way; there's no other possibility.

JA: We're talking about many things at once, and I know you're very tired at the end of the day. It's OK?

DL: I'm quite fresh.

JA: You're quite fresh? Excellent. OK. Would you give a little detail from your personal experience so that people could identify with these abstract topics. For instance, you've spent much of your lifetime meditating; engaged in actual practice. What is your personal experience of the nature of the mind?

DL: Its entity, or its nature, is that it is illuminating and knowing. Through the casting of an object's image, it is generated into that—into knowing that. The consciousness knows that object by way of being generated in its image, like a reflection. Now, for different Buddhist schools, there's a disagreement over whether the object exists externally or not. In other words, whether the object exists as a different substantial entity from the consciousness that knows it.

JA: *Does it?*

DL: Some say it does, and some say it doesn't.

JA: *To tie it all back to the beginning, again. On the one hand, we have this illuminating knowing thing called mind, which is beginningless, and on the other, we have matter. What's the universal, cosmologic connection between these two?*

DL: There's one kind of space that has the nature of lightness and darkness. This space is that of area—like what appears to our eyes. There's another space which is just a mere negative; an absence of obstructive contact. The latter one is permanent and thus, unchanging. There are however, causes and conditions for the former type of space. Hence you have to posit its continuum as beginningless, since it must arise from concordant, or similar causes. The space that I was speaking about earlier—that which serves as the basis of wind—and this one, which is impermanent but the continuum of which is beginningless, are probably the same. I can't explain this thoroughly. I think it would be impossible or difficult to say that consciousness arose from matter or that matter arose from consciousness.

JA: *Why?*

DL: Though it is in dependence upon the mind's being tamed or not tamed that actions are done which can have results in the material world of substances, when you talk about the continuation—the whole continuum of those substances—it is difficult to say that it's produced from consciousness. Also, if consciousness were produced from matter, then at times when there is no matter—such as during the aeons of vacuity following the destruction of a world system—there would be no sentient beings. This would contradict reason.

JA: Let me somehow try and make a bridge to the western way of thought with this. Twenty-six years ago, scientists confirmed that one chemical, DNA, produces all types of life on this planet. By recombining four chemical bases in infinite length and variety, DNA produces living forms. What does this evoke for you? What, if any, significance do you see in it?

DL: You are talking about very fine particles, right? These very fine, very minute particles, cannot be seen directly by the eye consciousness. Correct? But nowadays, in dependence upon technology, people are able to discover these very subtle things, and they are being found to be physical. They are very subtle, disintegrating moment by moment, but they can be found.

JA: But DNA itself—life—what is the life that is in the chemical? Is it consciousness; is that what life is, consciousness?

DL: DNA is probably not consciousness. It doesn't have to be that everything that moves about has consciousness. Trees have shape and movement and the particles inside rocks are moving about.

JA: But within DNA itself, it's very apparent that there's a certain organizing intelligence which is recombining these genes—these coded chemicals. Some mind is at work in DNA.

DL: If DNA was necessary for consciousness, then the child's consciousness would have to come from the parents, and there's no way that could be true. That just isn't the case.

JA: Well then, let's not speak in terms of individual beings, but in larger dimensions. There is an inanimate planet, and upon it appears this chemical which begins to produce beings in many different forms. It continues to grow and change over many millions of years. What intelligence is organizing the course of this evolution?

What is at work here? Would it be collective karma?

DL: Oh, yes.

JA: Can you say more about that?

DL: There is collective karma and specific karma.

JA: OK.

DL: The collective karma involved in this world system is not just that of humans, but of every type of sentient being—bugs and so forth—in the system. If four people set their hands on this table, the table becomes an object used by the four in common. Thus, this action causes them to accumulate a karma in common, the fruition of which they will experience in the future. Now, those things which one uses individually, they are based on—as well as produce—one's own individual karma.

JA: In other words, you're saying that DNA is the product of both the collective and individual karma of all the beings in this world system, through which they then manifest themselves?

DL: I've not had the opportunity to look into DNA in detail, to study it. It is matter; it is an object of comprehension by an eye consciousness. Can you see it through a microscope?

JA: Absolutely. Yes. There are sixty-four chromosomes on which it is collected for a human being. On each, it is arrayed in thousands of combinations called genes.

DL: It's physical. Once it's physical, then it has parts to it and directions. There's no way for it to be partless. If it were partless, if anything were partless, then there wouldn't be any form. The form couldn't be there. It probably doesn't have consciousness, but serves as a basis of consciousness.

JA: If it doesn't have consciousness itself, what is the cause which establishes it in a correct manner to manifest consciousness? If you said that originally consciousness does not manifest matter, then

45

what exactly is it that produces this inanimate DNA, which in turn manifests consciousness?

DL: This would be similar to the sense power of an eye. That is matter; it is not consciousness, yet it serves as a basis of consciousness and by doing so is a cause of consciousness. For instance, the brain. It's not consciousness, yet it serves as the basis of consciousness. Once something is a consciousness, it is necessarily not shape and color. However, as I mentioned earlier today, in dependence upon the power of meditative stabilization, samadhi,[15] you can achieve or create a higher order within a physical level. There are two types of this: that which can be observed by the senses, and that which can be perceived only by the mental consciousness. There are subtle physical things which can only be known by the mental consciousness. Thus there is fire and water that is produced by the power of meditative stabilization and yet, they are really not fire and water for they are produced in dependence on samadhi only. But they can perform the function of burning or making something wet.

JA: Where is this fire you're talking about?

DL: It is produced by a person who is capable of cultivating it: fire, water, wind and so forth. This is similar to a photograph that a person has imprinted with a mental image, which we saw earlier today. This is like that.

JA: So at a certain degree of control of the mind, physical things can be manifested?

DL: Yes.

JA: To what purpose?

DL: Just depends on one's motivation.

JA: I see. I'd like to ask you about something related to this. Since you were a little boy, you've been very interested in science. Why?

DL: Why? It is my wish. Well, let's see. I looked at many pictures, and then from that, I got interested. I had a lot of curiosity as a child.

And as you extend the "hows" back, that's how you get interested in science.

JA: *Looking for a root cause or something like that?*

DL: If you look for the root cause, then that's not science. Science comes after the root cause.

JA: *Halfway through your life you came out of a world where there was no technology into the middle of the twentieth century. Which developments, discoveries, have impressed or interested you most?*

DL: Again, today, this scanning machine. That is something special. Body scanning; it takes every centimeter of your body in cross-section. Very marvelous.

JA: *Why did that one interest you?*

DL: Hm? Very beneficial.

JA: *For that reason, it was the most intriguing?*

DL: There's no need to operate on the person to get the picture.

JA: *Some of these machines are making a lot of trouble for people- as well as helping them. What do you think the best way to use technology is?*

DL: That depends on motivation. Moderation and kindness. It'll go alright; that's it.

JA: *How do you feel about nuclear energy?*

DL: Good. I think it is good.

JA: *Why?*

DL: Because it helps. If you use it properly, I think so.

JA: *You feel that the possible benefit outweighs the danger?*

DL: Everything is a dependent-arising. You see, whether nuclear power is absolutely of benefit; of course not. But we have a difficult topic. You cannot determine that nuclear energy is bad on the basis of itself alone, because if you do that, then you'll just be an extremist yourself. If you go to any one extreme, it could be harmful.

JA: *What do you think about the broader, spiritual implications of nuclear power? We've tapped the energy in the atom, and with this most fundamental force—nothing less—we might well destroy our world. Do you see anything ironic in that?*

DL: Again, this just depends on your skill in knowing how to use nuclear energy. For instance, with respect to diet, if you don't know how to eat properly, you might kill yourself.

JA: *Going back to what we were discussing before; existence, and the evolution of the universe. Western science has shown that life on this planet developed from simple forms to highly sophisticated ones. Can you equate this linear evolution with the Buddhist view of cyclic existence in which beings migrate in an essentially circular pattern through the same basic life forms?*

DL: According to the scriptures I mentioned earlier, we also believe in both a highly developed state which slowly degenerates and a primitive one which evolves. Otherwise, I don't know. It's difficult to say. We have to investigate this further. I feel that different things could exist together. What science has found the present nature of evolution to be could be true, and at the same time, another type of evolution could also exist. It's difficult to say.

JA: *Is there a specific date, a fixed point or period set down in the scriptures, when cyclic existence, time and space, will be emptied of all beings?*

DL: According to one Buddhist scripture, it is explained this way. If you dig down one thousand yards into the earth and then dig around one thousand square yards and then fill this space with hairs a half inch long each; if you then throw away one hair every hundred years; when you are done, that will be the length of one intermediate aeon—one of the eighty. So like that.

JA: Does it say how many great aeons there are going to be?

DL: Oh, limitless. There is no limit to the maha or great aeons. The existence of this kind of earth disintegrates, begins to take form, and disintegrates again everywhere in the universe.

JA: So there is no fixed point when samsara, cyclic existence, will cease? It is said, isn't it, that samsara is beginningless, but it will have an end?

DL: Individually, it can end. Collectively, it is beginningless and endless. If you examine an individual person, there exists the possibility to bring to an end the causes which produce that person's samsaric existence. Therefore, there will be an end. But now, when we speak of the whole of samsara, then it is difficult to say because it has no limit. So something which is limitless—how can you put a time on it? That's the problem.

JA: A final question—the life forms we see around us are primarily broken into two types. One is plant, the other animal. Plants survive through the medium of their own beings, from sunlight, earth and air. Animals, though, have to take food from the outside and usually by killing others. Do you see any meaning, any spiritual signficance to the fact that life exists in these two ways?

DL: (Loud laughter) That is difficult. According to Buddhism, there might be a difference based on whether it is a sentient being or not.

JA: Are plants sentient beings? Do they have consciousness?

DL: Generally as a plant, no. But now again, there is a further complication. What is a real plant and what is something animal? That is difficult. These plants around us may be real plants. In that case, we would consider them not to have consciousness. There are some kinds of plants however, where it is difficult to say if it has consciousness or not. Even if you take the human body; when you break down the cells I'm not sure which kind don't have consciousness and which do. According to Buddhist texts, there are about eighty thousand cells with consciousness, eighty thousand sentient beings in the body, including worms. I think it's impossible for the human body to contain eighty thousand worms, which could be seen with the naked eye, but as I said, everything that moves doesn't necessarily have consciousness.

V.

Cyclic Existence And Sentient Beings

JA: How do you feel about Buddhism coming to America and the West?

DL: Religion has no boundaries. There are some Americans who are interested in it, and if it helps them, then that's sufficient.

JA: In general, it's not just interest in Buddhism, but there's been something of a spiritual renaissance in this country in the past 15 years. What do you think has caused this?

DL: It could be due to materialistic progress, and American culture is a mixture of many cultures. Therefore, Americans are very open to anything. There must be many factors, and there is much competition for jobs and so forth. Thus, people come to meet with difficulties, and out of that get interested in something serious. They go deeper, you see.

JA: From difficulty comes an interest in spiritual growth?

DL: If the mind is very restless, then just to meditate on one point or one subject for a short while will create some calm. In the beginning people became attracted to this kind of thing because it was like going on a mental picnic or vacation. And it was not just Buddhism, but all Eastern religions.

JA: What do you think of cults; people forfeiting their individuality to a religious figurehead or authority?

DL: To answer that, I'll talk about the Buddhist way of viewing a teacher. The doctrines that Buddha taught were not for the sake of displaying his knowledge to others, but in order to help them. Therefore, no matter what his own thought or realization was, he taught in accordance with the disposition, interest, and so forth of the listener. Those who follow Buddha's word, in order to determine his final meaning, must make a differentiation between that which is interpretable—as it was spoken for a specific purpose—and that which is definitive or incontrovertably true. If in differentiating what is interpretable and what is definitive, one had to rely on another scripture, then one would have to rely on a scripture to validate that scripture and a further one to validate the latter. It would then be limitless. Therefore, once one asserts that there is this differentiation, it is necessary to rely on reasoning to implement it. That which is not damaged by reasoning is definitive. Since this is the case, Buddha set forth the four reliances. Rely not on the person, but on the doctrine. With respect to the doctrine, rely not on the words, but on the meaning. With respect to the meaning, rely not on the interpretable meaning, but on the definitive meaning. With respect to the definitive meaning, one should rely not on comprehension by an ordinary state of consciousness, but on understanding by an exalted wisdom consciousness. Because of this, the reliability of teachings cannot be determined by considering the person who taught them, but by investigating the teachings themselves. In sutra, Buddha said "Monks and scholars should accept my word not out of respect, but upon analyzing it as a goldsmith analyzes gold, through cutting, melting, scraping and rubbing it." One doesn't determine that Buddha is a reliable source of refuge[16] by the fact that his body was adorned with major or minor marks, but because his teachings for the achievement of high status and definite goodness[17] are reliable. Since the teachings regarding high status touch on matters that involve very hidden phenomena[18] and are beyond the ordinary processes of reasoning, it is necessary to examine Buddha's teachings for the achievement of definite goodness. Specifically, these are the teachings regarding the realization of the wisdom of emptiness. Through determining that they are correct and incontrovertable, one can come to the conclusion that the teachings regarding high status are as well. As Dharmakirti says, a teacher must be one who is skilled in which behavior is to be adopted and which discarded. One cannot accept a teacher because that person performs miracles, has the clairvoyant ability to see things in the distance or is able to create certain physical emanations. Whether one can see far in the distance or not, doesn't matter. What matters is whether one knows the techniques for achieving happiness—as Dharmakirti says. If it were sufficient to be able to see things at a distance, then one should go for refuge to a vulture. (This is in the root stanzas of the *Pramanavarttika*[19] itself.) Now, this is all to show that a teacher who explains what is to be adopted and discarded must be fully qualified. Therefore, Buddha set forth in detail the qualifications for many different levels of teachers:

within the vinaya or discipline scriptures, within the sutras and within the various divisions of the tantras. It's very important before one accepts a teacher to analyze them, to see if he or she has these qualifications. It is particularly important in tantric practice. In one tantra, it says that since there is great danger for both the master and the student, it is necessary to analyze before-hand even if it takes twelve years to come to a conclusion. Now, if in Buddhism it were sufficient just to have faith, then Buddha would not have needed to set forth such great detail concerning the choice of a teacher. In mantric practice—tantra—guru yoga[20] is very important. But even though it is important, it doesn't operate on the basis of blind faith. It says in the discipline that if a lama teaches contrary to the doctrine one should object to it. A sutra quoted in Tsongkapa's *Great Exposition of the Stages of The Path*,[21] says that one should rely on a lama by agreeing with what is concordant with the doctrine and opposing that which is discordant. This is in a sutra in the Bodhisattva Pitaka. Then with respect to mantra, Ashvaghosha's *Fifty Stanzas on the Guru* states that if a lama says something which one cannot accept, one should verbally explain to him why. This describes how one is to rely on a lama within the three vehicles of Buddhism.[22] One shouldn't fall to either of the extremes. As in all practices, after ascertaining the truth with reason, one should then have faith, but that isn't a blind faith leading you into a chasm. You should examine what the teacher says, accepting what is suitable and rejecting that which is not. This is the general Buddhist procedure, and I agree with it. I follow it.

JA: How can you really go for refuge to either the teacher or the Buddha unless you yourself have already experienced the validity of their teaching?

DL: If one speaks about refuge with valid cognition, then it would be necessary to ascertain nirvana before going for refuge. In order to ascertain both the existence of nirvana and that it is obtainable, it is necessary to realize emptiness. This would be the mode of procedure for one who follows the facts; who has to get down to the facts. However, for other types of people, who mainly follow through faith, there are many different ways in which they generate belief. Thus, even if one had not gotten valid cognition regarding nirvana and its obtainability, at least one would have to have a correct assumption concerning it.

JA: Isn't it a contradiction to say that the followers of fact have to travel the whole path before taking refuge in the very path they would have then already traveled?

DL: The actualization of nirvana and the ascertainment that it exists are very different. For instance, actually arriving at this place and ascertaining that this place exists are different.

JA: The vast majority of people in the world are not actively engaged in spiritual development. The most important or deepest aspects of their lives are their relationships with others—particularly family members. To what degree do you think these basic relationships serve as a means for human growth? Do they function at all on their own to help people evolve?

DL: I don't know. One kind of love which we possess is the right kind of love. This can extend towards spiritual development. It can be used as the basis for the development of infinite kindness. So from that viewpoint, yes, the family life or family ties can benefit. In human nature, we already have a certain type of kindness. Part of that is reasonable. Now at the same time, this usual kindness that comes with human nature is strongly influenced by attachment. Now that has nothing to do with the spiritual side, and in fact, acts as an obstruction.

JA: Love, based on attachment?

DL: Yes.

JA: Can you talk about the right kind of love?

DL: There are many reasons for it. When you have pity or compassion for a very poor man, at that moment you are showing sympathy because he is poor. That love is based on right reasons. Now, the love towards your wife, your children, or a close friend is love based on an object of attachment. Once your attachment changes, then that kindness no longer exists. The other kind of love is not based on your attachment, but is love—as in this case—because a man is suffering from poverty. So as long as he suffers from poverty, your love will remain.

JA: Are you saying that the correct love is found only in empathy?

DL: Yes. It is similar. The right kind of love will not change according to your emotional feelings towards the object. Love that is connected with attachment will fluctuate very much according to how you look at it.

JA: Buddhists believe that the emotions are obscurations—mental defilements—which should be abandoned. In the West, though, one major criteria for a full life is just how deeply feelings are experienced. If passion is avoided, one feels a person is superficial. On the other hand, people often admire someone who has richly experienced life. Must these two views negate each other?

DL: This is a little complicated. Certain strong emotions come into you because of your attachment. Similarly, strong feelings can even enter into your practice of Dharma or your attitude towards your guru. Although the emotion might seem good, if someone is practicing properly, at a later stage he has to get rid of these feelings.

JA: So there really is no way to equate the two views? What if someone's friend or parent dies, don't you think it's good for them to feel sad?

DL: At the death of a parent or anyone else, there is a reason for being sad. I don't find much wrong in this. If something unfortunate happened to your own parents or someone for whom you've had much love, there is a good reason to feel sad. Now here, if someone loses their parents and is sad, I think their sadness should be based on reasoning—no more, no less. I think that is correct. No less means he feels very sorry. No more, he accepts it. Now you see, the sadness which is based on strong attachment is bad. Because of that sadness people may even kill themselves. Going to that extent is beyond reason.

JA: So that is what should be abandoned?

DL: Yes.

JA: Can you describe what type of mental phenomena dreaming is?

DL: There are techniques for causing dreams to become non-mistaken as to the ultimate nature of reality. Otherwise, dreams, though there are unusual ones, are of little value in developing the mind.

JA: Is it just because the mind is so restless that even when the body sleeps, it continues to function?

DL: When one is sleeping without dreams—in a dreamless state—there is less conceptuality. When dreams appear, one generates desire, hatred and so forth; and then of course, there is a lot of conceptuality. A dream consciousness is easier to change or transform. The experience of pleasure and pain in it can influence the same experience by a coarser consciousness when awake. Because a dream consciousness is more subtle than a waking consciousness, it is more effective. But now, a special dream body is a case of the coarse body actually being left. There are cases of this due to one's former actions or karma, like a gift at birth, a talent. These people can experience what is actually going on at this time externally—beyond their bodies. There are also cases of people who train in making use of the special dream body. Not to lose time in their religious practice, they often spread the pages of a book out before going to sleep. During sleep they then depart from their bodies and spend that time reading. The pages would be separated before because the dream body is incapable of moving coarse physical matter.

JA: Could you elucidate from a Buddhist point of view, exactly what happens on a physiologic basis, during the whole course of cyclic existence; life, death and rebirth?

DL: There are four states. The birth state is said to be momentary, just at the point of conception. The next moment is the beginning of the prior time state, ranging from when the coarse body starts to form until death. Then during the death state, even though it is taking place within the old body, the relationship of support and supporter of consciousness abiding in the body has been severed. At the point of death, the relationship of consciousness supported by a physical base, takes place only on the subtlest level. At this point, individual consciousness is conjoined with the subtlest inner energy or "air," as it says. For one who is going to pass through the intermediate or bardo states, as soon as the death state stops, the intermediate state begins. In the intermediate states although one doesn't have a gross physical body, one does have a form—achieved through the interaction of inner air and consciousness. It is grosser than the most subtle body, but more subtle than the usual physical one we see.

JA: Does this have a shape?

DL: Oh, yes. It will have the shape of the being which one will be reborn as. There are systems, however, which say that for the first half of the period of the intermediate state, the bardo body has the form of the past life, and for the next half, that of the life to come. Every seven days there is a small death which takes place to the bardo body. With seven such deaths occurring every seven days, it is possible to remain in the intermediate state for up to seven weeks, but no more. By that time one will definitely take rebirth. Beings in the intermediate state are like gods or spirits in that they do not have a gross physical body susceptible to many limitations. They can't be seen by ordinary sight. Among all those who do not have gross bodies—not just bardo dwellers—there are many different types: gods, demigods, spirits, etc. As in human society there are those who have no contact with Buddhist practice, those who have a little contact, some more, some less. The oracles[23] generally speaking, are people like us, within cyclic existence. Such beings as Chenrezi among the society of gods, are persons who have already obtained enlightenment. Now there are many different types of Chenrezis. The compassion of all Buddhas in general, its manifestation in form, is called Chenrezi. Thus, this type of Chenrezi is not an individual being. However, just as Shakyamuni is a specific person, there is also a Chenrezi who is a specific person. Also, there are people like us who might take Chenrezi as a special deity. When that person becomes enlightened, he or she will appear in the form of Chenrezi. Because the person at the time of the stage of generation in Highest Yoga Tantra[24] generated his or her self as such, he is designated with the name Chenrezi. However, they don't have to continue appearing just as Chenrezi. Simultaneously, they may appear in many different ways. From a Buddha's own point of view one can only say that a Form Body is a final or highest Form Body.[25] One cannot say that inwardly it is one way or another. It appears simultaneously in many different forms in accordance with the needs of the trainees[26] and in dependence upon that Buddha's former wishes and prayers.

Therefore, one Buddha would appear automatically and at the same time in the aspect of Chenrezi, Manjusri, Maitreya[27] and so forth, according to the needs of the trainee.

JA: In connection with this, you know the story of Jesus Christ. What do you think about it?

DL: Though one couldn't say definitely, it would seem that this was a case of an enlightened being manifesting in an appropriate way to lead others on. It is definite, though, that he was a superior being.

JA: These manifestations that appear like reflections in physical form of a higher being; do they have a sense of "I," a relative sense of self?

DL: There are many possibilities. For instance, a Bodhisattva who is able to do emanations could emanate himself as a certain being. Then that being would have a sense of "I." However, if that being in turn emanated out another form, then that one would appear to be a person, but wouldn't be. So there are many cases. Some have a sense of "I," and some do not.

JA: The second emanation would be an actual body with an actual consciousness, but would not have a sense of "I"?

DL: The secondary one could perform the function of a human being, but wouldn't be a separate person. For instance, if an enlightened being emanated a hundred forms at one time, there would not be a hundred persons, there would still just be the one central being.

JA: Would the central emanator be simultaneously cognizant of everything occurring to the one hundred manifestations?

DL: There are different levels here. For those of lower realization, it would be necessary for the central emanator to control each one separately. For those of higher realization, the emanations can control themselves. The factor of spontaneity and acting without exertion is involved here. It is the difference in where the control is. When one can spontaneously emanate forms without exertion, then each of the emanations is under his or her own control.

JA: Is such a person simultaneously aware of its own self as well as its existence as an emanation?

DL: Yes. There are cases in which among one hundred emanations, each one knows what the other ones are doing. Certainly for a Buddha or a high Bodhisattva, this is true. But this is difficult to explain. Until one experiences it oneself, one might think that this was just talking about something that was senseless. Something like science fiction or religious fiction (laughter).

JA: To what degree do you feel the tulku[28] system as it existed in Tibet was accurate? How many incarnate lamas discovered in the past do you think were genuine?

DL: Oh, that is difficult. There are two things that are very important in this. One is that examining the tulku should be done very thoroughly. It's very easy for this examination or investigation not to be done properly. Secondly, we have got to see how the tulku leads his life. We have to judge by that also. The very purpose of voluntarily reincarnating is to produce some good result. Without that good result, then it is doubtful. The reincarnation takes rebirth with choice, intentionally, deliberately, with the definite purpose of serving humanity through religious or other means. Anyway, there must be some concrete result. In some cases where there is not this result, then I am doubtful. So I think fifty-fifty. It might be a little presumptuous on my part to say this.

JA: I know it's hard to generalize. How has it worked since you have come into exile in terms of discovering incarnations?

DL: There are still a few who are being recognized. Some are quite authentic. Mainly it is the child's own behavior: showing some significant signs.

JA: It's had, of course, to decrease in number; is that right?

DL: Quite a lot! In the past you see, there was a population of six million. Now there is only one hundred thousand. If you compare, I think it has decreased quite a lot (laughter). We have some American lamas, also (laughter).

JA: *What do you mean?*

DL: Yes. At least two, I think, recognized as Tibetan lamas.

JA: *Can you say a little bit about them?*

DL: I don't know much.

JA: *How can the certification process be applied to them? In the same way?*

DL: Maybe they themselves investigate it. I don't know the details.

JA: *You, yourself, don't approve them?*

DL: I have nothing to do with this.

JA: *I'd like to draw a parallel to what you were saying about one being emanating numerous forms. There are supposed to be about 100 trillion cells in the human body. Each cell performs functions that seem to indicate it has an individual consciousness. Yet they are all under the control of the same body. Could all sentient beings be related in a like manner, as parts of one organism? In other words, as components or emanations of a single body?*

DL: All sentient beings are of the same taste—in the sense of being the same type—in that the nature of their consciousness is mere illumination and knowing. Otherwise, they are not connected. If you suppose that many sentient beings come out of one source like a God, the answer is no.

JA: *You feel that they are independent of one another?*

DL: Yes. They are separate. Even when they are enlightened, they remain separate though their realization is the same.

JA: *What do you think is the nature of the consciousness of the 100 trillion cells?*

DL: Wouldn't there be a body consciousness pervading them

throughout? For instance, where the eye sense is, within that matter, the eye consciousness holds or occupies that area. At the same time so does the body consciousness. The body consciousness pervades throughout the body.

JA: In each of these human cells, as we discussed before, there are thousands of genes, little pieces of chemical code that determine the nature of the whole body as well as the particular function of the cell they inhabit. Now within each cell the complete code for the whole human being is contained, yet only one gene is activated to produce the required form for its position, such as a toenail or eye or finger cell. What determines, do you think, the fact that the exact gene is activated and no other?

DL: This is a physical function. It's body, not consciousness. It's held by consciousness, but the body performs the action.

JA: Before you stated that the mind and hence, beings, are beginningless. How far back then, does the memory of a sentient being go? Endlessly?

DL: For people who are untrained, the more one's consciousness becomes subtle—such as at death—the more one becomes less aware. For one who is trained to utilize these consciousnesses, however, one has much greater awareness and much greater memory as the subtler states manifest. Among some people that I know, when a more subtle consciousness is produced, they are clearly able to remember seven, eight hundred, a thousand years back—with that consciousness.

JA: How far does the memory go back? Infinitely?

DL: To go back a very long period of time, it is not sufficient merely to generate and utilize a subtle form of consciousness. For times way, way back, it is necessary to remove all the obstructions to omniscience. I am referring to super, super sensory objects far off in time and place. For instance, even though he had great clairvoyance, Shariputra did not know about a very subtle root of virtue that was in a particular trainee, but Buddha did. Maudgalyayana's[29] mother was in an extremely distant place in space and time and he didn't know where she was, but Buddha did. Since objects can be super, super sensory in respect to time or place, it is not enough just to manifest a subtle consciousness. One has to overcome the obstructions to omniscience, too.

JA: Are you saying that when those obstructions are overcome, both space and time are eliminated—that the knowledge of events everywhere in the universe; past, present, and future is simultaneous with their occurrence?

DL: Time and space are relative. They are relative to a particular consciousness. What for us would be a year, for someone who has manifested a subtler consciousness, would be a shorter period of time. Also, it is possible for a person who has obtained great meditative stabilization to transform or change a moment into an aeon or an aeon into a moment—that is, for himself or herself only.

JA: Where is memory stored?

DL: It is not just in the brain. At such times as we are discussing, it is not necessary to have a brain. Consciousness alone can apprehend the past events. It must be with the subtle consciousness. For example, when the subtle mind of clear light[30] manifests at death, the brain is already finished. From the point of view of its cognition, it's called consciousness, and from the point of view of its engaging, or moving to its object, it's called inner air or energy. The very subtle air and consciousness are one undifferentiable entity. They are one entity differentiated only for thought or by way of their opposites.

JA: Within this energy-consciousness are there traces or imprints which contain all the memories? Is this very moment being imprinted onto that?

DL: Yes. If you remember your last lifetime, the brain of that lifetime is no longer around, and this brain is new, right? So the picture can only be imprinted in the consciousness. This is similar to what the president of the University of Virginia described to me concerning the complete change of brain cells every several years.

JA: This most subtle consciousness-energy, is that what defines a sentient being as separate? Is this the ultimate demarcation point between one person and another?

DL: There is a mere "I" which is designated in dependence upon the continuum of consciousness. There are two types of "I" or self: coarser and more subtle. There is the "I" which is designated on the gross mind and body and that which is designated on the subtle mind and energy. When the one is active, the other is not.

JA: Is the mind involved with the most subtle energy that which is beginningless, or is it a secondary function of the energy-consciousness imputed back on itself?

DL: The very subtle mind and energy is the base of designation for the subtle "I." When you speak of designating the "I" to this energy-mind, it's not necessary that the designator actually be among them. Someone once asked a question of a great geshay. He said that if a person was in a house looking at a pillar, that pillar could be designated to exist by thought, and he could understand that, but when no one was in the house, how could the pillar be designated? So the geshay said, "Yes, it does seem difficult." Now, as soon as the questioner left, the geshay turned to a friend nearby and said, "Well, this person seems to think that a designating consciousness has to be wrapped around and tied up with every object." So you see, it means this. The fact that a designated object cannot be found to ultimately exist when sought in analysis, means that necessarily the object is just designated by a conceptual consciousness. Now, when you examine whether it is designated by this or that person's conceptual consciousness, ultimately you won't find that either. This constitutes a mode of ultimate analysis of something's being conceptually designated. You won't be able to find it. Thus, that things are conceptually designated is also without inherent existence. It's also empty.

JA: I'm not sure I understand. Is the "I" the subtle mind?

DL: The coarse "I" is designated in dependence on the coarse mind and body. But even when they are not operating, there has to be an "I" designated. That is then designated to the subtle mind and body which are then present. For instance, a highly developed yogi who is able to manifest a subtler consciousness and at the same time view conventional phenomena, for that person there is an innate sense of "I"—not in the coarser sense, but in a far more subtle sense—designated upon the subtle mind and body. There is nothing else to posit. If either the very subtle mind or energy were posited as the "I," itself, then there would be the fault that is set forth in Nagarjuna's *Treatise On The Middle Way,* that agent and object would be one, designator and designatee, the appropriator and the appropriated. For instance, when you say, "my mind," the controller or the owner is the "I." In the case you are describing, the owner and owned would be one—impossible. If you posited one of those as actually being the "I," this fault would be incurred. Because of this, it's not the case.

JA: What happens to the most subtle energy-mind, when a being becomes enlightened?

DL: The "I" of a Buddha, the self of a Buddha, is this subtle "I." At the level of Buddhahood there is no coarse wind and mind. All of the five sense activities are done by the subtle energy and consciousness itself. Because that is all there is. It has become an omniscient consciousness. So at the time of the final vajra-like meditative stabilization of a learner,[31] one passes through in the forward process the four consciousnesses[32] and then just the mind of clear light is left; one doesn't manifest ever again the coarser levels of consciousness. Thus, there would only be the subtle "I" which is designated on the subtlest mind. For instance, for Shakyamuni Buddha, who appeared with a coarse mind and body that we could meet with, for him you could posit a coarse "I"—but just the appearance of such.

JA: Let me just ask you something else about the process of memory. When the human embryo develops, it goes through all the stages of evolution; fish, mammal, etc., that have led to human beings. Why do you think it has to repeat every stage?

DL: It is due to the five fundamental and five secondary winds or currents of energy which control the human form. It must have something to do with the actual formation of these winds in the new body, but I do not know this well.

JA: And the memory of those past creations is inherent in each of these energy currents as they produce the physical forms?

DL: The very subtle wind refers to the very subtle form of the life-bearing wind. The upwards-moving wind has a relation with speech, spitting, and so forth. The pervasive wind has a function throughout the body. The fire-accompanying wind has the function of digestion of food and increase of the body's elements. The downwards-voiding wind has to do with the increase, holding and letting go of seminal fluid, blood, feces, urine, and so forth. I haven't remembered this well so take care.[33]

VI.

Emptiness: The Two Truths

JA: Can you explain why Buddhists believe the mind is obscured; why we have been beginninglessly ignorant?

DL: There are different types of obscurations. In one way, there are two. The first is an obscuration of not knowing. The second is a case of misconceiving. If you ask from what an obscuration arises, it comes from the continuation of former moments of obscuration. If you seek another explanation, then there would have to be a first moment to obscuration. In this case there would be a contradiction with reasoning. As it says in Aryadeva's *Four Hundred,* "Though there is no beginning to afflictive emotions, there is an end." Because ignorant consciousnesses misconceive objects, there is an end to them. They can be stopped by right understanding, but since they are generated as continuations of former moments of that type of consciousness, there is no beginning to them.

JA: Why is the mind not inherently enlightened?

DL: Once it has defilements—is together with defilements—it can't be that it was once without them. Still, because the basic entity of the mind is always unfabricated and clear, it is indeed thoroughly good. Therefore, it is called thoroughly good: Samantabhadra.[34] It would contradict reasoning to propound that the mind is first pure and then later became adventitiously defiled. Thus, it can only be said that from the very start the mind is defiled.

JA: Why is the enlightened nature just a seed? Why is it not thoroughly developed?

DL: Because it is a seed its fruition is yet to occur. The fact that any consciousness is established as having a nature of mere illumination and knowing, and that that factor is capable of turning into enlightenment is designated with the name, 'seed'. There is nothing more than that. If there was, you'd have to say that a God created it. Then you would have to explore the nature of God: investigate whether the nature of God had a beginning or end. There are many such investigations in the ninth chapter of Shantideva's *Engaging in the Bodhi-*

sattva's Deeds as well as Dharmakirti's *Commentary on Dignaga's "Compendium on Valid Cognition."* I am not criticizing those who assert a creator God. I am explaining the Buddhist viewpoint. If there are many internal contradictions in a doctrine, revealed by reasoning, then one should drop that doctrine and choose one which doesn't have such discrepancies. As it says in the fourth reliance, rely not on knowledge but on exalted wisdom. There are many phenomena which are not understood until one advances in mental development. There are many unusual phenomena which we cannot explain now with this type of consciousness.

JA: Can you explain how the other mental afflictions stem, or come out of innate ignorance?

DL: As I said, there are two types of ignorance. The first is a mere obscuration with respect to the status of phenomena. The other is ignorance which misconceives the nature of phenomena. The latter one conceives that phenomena inherently exist, which they don't. Within this misconception of inherent existence, there are again two types: conceptions of persons as inherently existent and conceptions of other phenomena as also such. This division is made by way of a consideration of users of objects and objects used. Within the conception of persons as inherently existent, there are cases of conceiving both one's own self and other selves to truly exist. Viewing the transitory collection of body and mind as a real "I" is a case of viewing your own self as inherently existent. With respect to this view, there are two further types. One is a conception that observes the transitory collection which gives rise to the thought of "I" and conceives it to inherently exist. Another observes "mine" and conceives it to exist in the same way. Now, first of all, one generates a conception of the inherent existence of those phenomena—the mental and physical aggregates—which serve as the basis of designation of the "I." After that thought, the "I" which is designated in dependence on mind and body is conceived to exist in its own right. Then, with that view of the transitory as the cause, one conceives "mine" to inherently exist. As Chandrakirti[35] says, "Initially there is attachment to the "I"—a self—and then attachment to mine." Once there is the class of self, there is the class of other. Once these two classes are distinguished, one becomes desirously attached to the class of self and hateful towards the class of other. From this, are generated all the other problems. For instance, due to the view of the transitory as an "I" which is inherently existent, one generates pride in oneself as superior to others. Then, even afflicted doubt—since it's a case of emphasizing the "I" which might not believe in something (the final reason being that 'I don't believe in such and such')—depends on this. And jealousy. Also, induced by this view of the "I" as inherently existent, are extreme views: views of permanence and views of annihilation. For example, believing that former and later births don't exist or believing that once there is a self that this self will exist forever. So first a phenomenon appears to inherently exist and when it does, its qualities of good, bad and whatever also appear to exist in this way. The mind then assents to that appearance. Since this is an appearance based on a superimposition of goodness and of badness—beyond that which is actually there—one's mind falls into extreme conceptions of genuine goodness and badness and the operation of improper attitudes, which, in turn, generate the afflictive emotions.

JA: *Could you describe the two truths: ultimate and conventional; what they are, and how they work?*

DL: This is important. Take the table as an example. If one searches for the object designated—the table itself—it can't be found. If one divides up the parts of the table in terms of directions or divides up its qualities or substances, then one can't find a whole which is the table. Indeed, to our minds there is a distinction between whole and parts such that when they appear to us, there seems to be a whole separate from parts—parts separate from whole. In reality, however, there isn't. Now, when one searches in this way, one will not find the table. This non-finding, though, does not mean that the table doesn't exist. We're using it right? But if we search for it, we can't find it. So there are two types of modes of being of the table. One is the positing of the table by a mind which doesn't analyze and is just involved in the conventionality. That sort of table is found by that sort of mind. However, if you take the table as the object, if you are not satisfied with just this which you put your hand on but search to discover what it actually is among the parts—whether this is it or that is it—then there isn't anything that can be found to be it. Why is there this non-finding of the table? It's because the table is something that is such that if analytically sought, it can't be found. Now what does the mind searching to find the table among its parts discover? It finds just that non-finding of the table. This non-finding itself is a quality of the table; its substratum or base. This non-finding is the final nature of the table. Something more subtle does not exist. Thus, this is the ultimate or final mode of establishment of the table. Now, this mode of being is sought with respect to the table as the base or substratum. Therefore, this non-finding is the actual mode of being of the table. Thus, with respect to the one basis, the table, there are two natures: one that is found by a non-analytical mind and one that is found by the analytical mind. With respect to one base, then, there is an object found by a consciousness distinguishing the ultimate and an object found by a consciousness distinguishing the conventional.[36] Thus it is said: "Form is emptiness. Emptiness is form." Now these two are mutually exclusive. The two truths are one entity but are mutually exclusive.

JA: How?

DL: With respect to a phenomenon, that which is its ultimate truth is not its conventional truth and visa versa.

JA: So, it's incorrect to say that they are mutually definitive?

DL: The one doesn't define the other. Still, if you take the ultimate reality or emptiness of the table as the substratum and search to see if it can be found; then it becomes a conventional truth in terms of itself as the substratum. In relation to the table, its emptiness is an ultimate truth, but in relation to its own reality, i.e., the reality of the reality, it's a conventional truth. It's contradictory for something to be its own mode of being. Therefore, the reality of something, is not its own reality. This is because when reality is sought, when the nature of things is sought, it can't be found either.

JA: When emptiness first appears to the mind, what is it like?

DL: Even though the word, dharmata,[37] doesn't have any negative particle in it, when that—the nature or reality of phenomena—appears to the mind, it must appear through the root of a negation. It is important to make this distinction. I'm talking within the context of the two truths as set forth in Nagarjuna's *Treatise on the Middle Way*. Is it that when inherent existence is sought, it is not found because it doesn't exist, or even though it exists, it isn't found because it can't be found under analysis? It is the former. When you look at how things appear to your mind, they appear as if they were such that they could be found upon analysis. Therefore, if things did exist in the way they appear to our minds, when you examine them they should become clearer and clearer. The fact that they do not, is a sign that they don't exist in the way they appear to. In sum, though they appear to inherently exist, they don't exist in that way. Now, in your mind, you initially have a sense that the object doesn't exist in the way it appears to. When you get used to this thought, accustomed to it, you eventually gain ascertainment that the object does not exist at all in the way it appears. At that time, your own sense of appearance is an experience of vacuity, which is simply the absence of inherent existence. At the beginning of this process, the object—this thing which is empty—might still appear. In an easy way, if one goes to a cinema, you might differentiate two different times while watching the movie. In both cases pictures would appear to your eye consciousness, but in the first instance one would just observe them, while in the latter you would be thinking strongly that this doesn't exist as a fact. If you strongly develop and maintain the thought that this doesn't exist—if you concentrate on its non-existence—then in time the appearance itself will begin to vanish. This is because the immediately preceding condition of the eye consciousness will begin to deteriorate. Therefore, when you initially ascertain emptiness, just a mere negative or absence of the object of negation—inherent existence—is ascertained. Even if at the beginning the object still appears; in time.with concentration just on emptiness, it will disappear. Then due to observing the emptiness of the object, when the object reappears, the thought that it doesn't exist in the way that it seems to, is induced. This is called the illusory-like appearance. At this point you are able to control your afflictive emotions. These faulty consciousnesses can in no way be produced without the assistance of the conception of inherent existence. Even though for beginners there are cases when the conception of inherent existence acts as an assistor to a virtuous consciousness, in general, it is not necessary that such a consciousness have assistance from the misconception of the nature of existence. Therefore, a consciousness realizing that objects do not exist in their own right serves to obstruct the generation of afflictions whereas it doesn't serve to obstruct a virtuous consciousness.

JA: *At the moment emptiness is understood—when the object vanishes—what does it feel like?*

DL: I'll just give a conventional example. For instance, the reflection of a face is empty of being a face, but its emptiness of being a face is not its reality; its emptiness of inherent existence is. When from the very depths the mind realizes the absence of this kind of existence of the object, at that point no other consciousness is being generated. Not even the thought, "this is emptiness." If you did think, "this is emptiness," then emptiness would be distant. It would be like an object under observation. It would not have arrived at being the actual object of apprehension by the consciousness.

JA: *So there is a loss of duality?*

DL: No. Even here there is still duality. There is the duality of the appearance of the conventional object as well as the appearance of the image of emptiness.

JA: *If you were to describe the image itself in conventional terms, would you say that it's clear, vacuous, buoyant, luminous?*

DL: That's very difficult to describe. To explain this exactly is very difficult. There are many different types of dualistic appearance. One is the appearance of conventionalities—objects as we normally see them. Then there is the appearance of inherent existence; also the appearance of subject and object as if different and the appearance of a general image—an image covering all objects in a particular group. When one gets used to the mind realizing emptiness—cultivating it even further in and out of meditative equipoise—and it turns into direct perception; then for that consciousness all types of dualistic appearance have vanished.

JA: *There is no natural luminosity or clarity to the appearance of emptiness?*

DL: No, but in terms of tantric practice it's a different story. That's not from the point of view of emptiness, but from the consciousness. Due to the dissolving of the coarser consciousnesses, there are many different types of appearances. These appearances result from the subtler consciousnesses as well as being connected to one's body; the white and red constituents and so forth.[38]

JA: Can you describe the mind of a Buddha?

DL: That which prevents the mind from knowing all there is to be known, are called the obstructions to omniscience. With respect to the obstructions to omniscience, there are potencies[39] which are established by the conception of inherent existence and which cause objects to appear as if they inherently or concretely exist. Even though primarily the false appearance of an object is the fault of the subject—the consciousness cognizing it—there may be some fault with the object in that it itself is polluted by ignorance or the latencies of ignorance. From this appearance—that of objects as inherently existent—there is the defilement which conceives the two truths to be different entities. Due to this defilement, when phenomena appear, they seem to exist in their own right, thus preventing the appearance of their reality. Similarly, when the reality of an object appears, the object cannot. We're talking about direct perception. When this obstruction to omniscience is removed, however, then while knowing the object one can know its nature and while knowing its nature, one can know the object. One mind can then simultaneously and directly ascertain both an object and its nature. Thus an omniscient consciousness—from the point of view of knowing conventional objects—is a consciousness which perceives the varieties of all phenomena. From the point of view of its knowing the nature of objects, it's a consciousness which knows the mode of being of objects, i.e., emptiness. But it is just one consciousness that knows both. This is a distinctive feature of the omniscient consciousness of a Buddha.

JA: Why is omniscience dependent on the elimination of the latencies through compassion?

DL: The reason for wanting to be omniscient is to help others. To do so, one must know how to help others. Thus, nothing can be obscured. Those defilements which obstruct knowledge of the different dispositions, interests and so forth of trainees, are the main enemy of a Bodhisattva. The obstructions to omniscience are never in any way helpful to a Bodhisattva, whereas the obstructions to liberation, that is to say the afflictions, can sometimes be helpful in achieving the welfare of others (as in the case of a leader's fathering many children to help in administration). For a viewing consciousness realizing emptiness to act as an antidote to the obstructions to omniscience depends greatly on motivation. Even though the view realizing emptiness in the continuum of a Listener or Solitary Realizer Superior, is the same as the view in the continuum of a Bodhisattva Superior, the ability of the latter to serve as an antidote to the obstructions to omniscience is due to motivation and also due to great merit.[40] There is no way for the collection of wisdom to be brought to completion without that of the collection of merit. It's as if you are going to put up one of these rafters here. To do so, you need to put up two pillars. Even though you don't need one pillar to put up the other, to hold up that rafter, both must be used. So in order for the view realizing emptiness to turn into the Truth Body of a Buddha, it is necessary for it to have all of the causes required for the production of a Form Body.

JA: How is it that compassionate means and the wisdom of emptiness[41] are ultimately identical?

DL: In the Perfection Vehicle[42] there is a description of wisdom and method conjoined. For example, before entering into meditative equipoise on emptiness, one generates an altruistic mind directed toward becoming enlightened. Then the meditative equipoise is conjoined with the force of that altruistic motivation. Also, when one is practicing altruistic acts—giving, ethics, and so forth[43] these should be conjoined with the force of the mind realizing emptiness. Thus in this way, there is a union of wisdom and method, the one affecting the other. In mantra, there is a union of method and wisdom within one consciousness and even more profound features of that union within Highest Yoga Tantra.

JA: How, in a Buddha's mind, is bliss united with this?

DL: Yes. There is a feeling of bliss. From a Buddha's own point of view everything is a pure appearance, and a blissful appearance. From his own point of view. Now, does suffering appear to a Buddha? Yes, but not from his own point of view; but due to its appearance in another person undergoing suffering. Does an appearance of inherent existence occur to a Buddha? Yes, but not from a Buddha's own viewpoint; but by way of its appearing to a person who hasn't abandoned the obstructions to omniscience. Now, the appearance of inherent existence does, in general, exist. Something's existing, and its not appearing to a Buddha is contradictory. Therefore, whatever exists must appear to a Buddha, but not necessarily from his own point of view. Through the force of its appearing to someone else and only through that does it appear.

Notes

1. See Bibliography

2. Mahakala (Tib. Nak-po-chen-po) is a wrathful emanation of Avalokiteshvara (Tib. Chenrezi), the Bodhisattva of Infinite Compassion, of whom the Dalai Lama is an incarnation. He is one of the primary protective deities of the Buddhist teaching.

3. Located near present-day Rajgir in Bihar, India, Nalanda was the largest of Mahayana Buddhism's monastic universities. It was founded in the 5th century by a Gupta king and destroyed during the Moslem invasions of the 12th and 13th centuries.

4. Predicted by the Buddha in several sutras, Nagarjuna was born in southern India around the 1st century A.D. He became one of the foremost exponents of the newly cohering Mahayana, as well as founding The Madhyamika School through six major works clarifying the emptiness of inherent existence as the final status of phenomena.

5. Dependent-arising (Sans. pratityasamūtpada; Tib. ten-jung) refers to the Buddhist doctrine of cause and effect in which phenomena and events are held to be produced and destroyed dependently, i.e., through causes and conditions.

6. Geshay literally means "spiritual friend," though it is most often translated Doctor of Buddhist Philosophy or Master of Metaphysics. The geshay degree, to which most monks of Tibet's largest sect—the Ge-luk-pa ("Wholesome Way") or Yellow Hats—aspire, requires extensive study of five major areas usually taking more than twenty years.

7. Before its destruction in the early 1960's by the Chinese, Drepung Monastery was the world's largest religious institution. Over 10,000 monks lived within its precincts, located five miles northwest of Lhasa.

8. Charles Bell, Great Britain's resident in Tibet, recounts the Dalai Lama's enthronement in his book, *Portrait of The Dalai Lama*.

9. Kyabjé Ling Rimpoché: the Dalai Lama's senior tutor and current head of the Ge-luk-pa Sect.

10. Shunyata (Tib. tong-pa-nyi) can be translated as either emptiness or voidness. It denotes the Buddhist conception of the ultimate nature of reality and refers specifically to the lack of an inherently existent self in all phenomena and beings.

11. Bodhichitta (Tib. chang-chub-gyi-sem) means mind of enlightenment. It is divided into two types: conventional and ultimate. Conventional bodhichitta is the altruistic motive to obtain enlightenment for the sake of freeing all sentient beings from suffering and also refers to the altruistic practices which this motive entails. Ultimate bodhichitta is the realization of ultimate truth or emptiness in the mental continuum of a Bodhisattva.

12. One of Tibet's three original provinces, Kham, lies east of Utsang (central Tibet) and south of Amdo (northeast Tibet). Following the formation of the Tibetan Autonomous

Region (TAR) in December, 1964, it was severed by Peking from Utsang and incorporated into the Chinese state of Szechuan. Amdo has also been cut off from central Tibet and is now treated as part of Tsinghai.

13 The *Abhidharmakosha* or "Treasury of Knowledge" was written by the Buddhist scholar, Vasubandhu, approximately 900 years after the Buddha's death. It deals extensively with the various classes of mental and physical phenomena, placing special emphasis on which traits are to be developed, and which abandoned in the quest for enlightenment.

14 The Tibetan term, lung (Sans. prana) can be translated as air (inner or outer), energy or wind.

15 Samadhi (Tib. ting-nge-dzin) means meditative stabilization, specifically one-pointed concentration on an object. There are nine levels leading to a fully qualified state of meditative stabilization called calm abiding (Sans. shamatha; Tib. zhi-gnas) which can be used as a basis for attaining supernormal or miraculous abilities.

16 Refuge refers to the Buddhist practice of "taking refuge" from the sufferings of cyclic existence (Sans. samsara; Tib. khor-wa) in The Three Jewels: The Buddha, Dharma and Sangha. The Buddha or "Awakened One" (Tib. Sang-gye) has realized both the ultimate and conventional nature of existence and is therefore a fit source of refuge from it. His teaching, the Dharma (Tib. chö), comprises the cessation of suffering as well as the path of inner development sentient beings must follow to obtain liberation. The Sangha or community (Tib. Ge-dun) are all those practicing the Dharma. Technically the term denotes any group of four or more fully ordained monks or a Bodhisattva who has obtained the first Bodhisattva stage (Sans. bhumi; Tib. sa) equivalent to the path of seeing.

17 High status indicates a high rebirth either as a human or god among the six realms of samsara. Definite goodness refers both to a state free of samsara and to Buddhahood.

18 Specifically cause and effect. Though cause and effect is the foundation of the Buddhist teachings, it is often impossible (with a normal consciousness) to recognize a specific cause or causes for a specific effect.

19 The *Pramanavarttika,* written by Dharmakirti around 500 A.D. is a compendium of teachings on correct or unmistaken knowledge. The two types of correct knowledge set forth in the text are correct inference or logic and direct perception. They apply to both conventional and ultimate truths.

20 Guru yoga entails a set of practices in which one's own teacher is viewed as the embodiment of the qualities of all the Buddhas. It is done for the purpose of enhancing awareness through mixing one's consciousness with an exalted object.

21 Tsong-ka-pa (1357-1419) founder of the Ge-luk-pa Sect, was born in Amdo on what later became the site of Kum Bum Monastery. He wrote over 200 books of which the *Lam Rim Chen-mo* or Stages On The Path To Enlightenment (extensive version) is one of the most widely studied.

22 See notes 42 and 40.

23 There were numerous oracles in Tibet; individuals—often self-proclaimed—who served as mediums for specific gods or spirits. Chief among them were the two State Oracles, Nechung and Ga-dong.

24 The stage of generation (Tib. kye-rim), particular to Annutara or Highest Yoga Tantra (the final and most sophisticated of the four Tantric cycles), involves practices through which the meditator, after having realized emptiness, projects or generates this wisdom consciousness into the form of a tutelary deity. During the practice, the full course of cyclic existence is duplicated within the mind of the meditator, i.e., death, intermediate state and rebirth. (The final one encompasses the actual generation into the deities' form.) These states both correspond to and devolve from specific types of consciousness. It is the meditator's goal to gain control over the latter, thereby effecting release from their concomitant conditions. At first, such an endeavor is merely imaginary; a mimicking of the consciousnesses, the states they create and one's own ascendency over them. The actual achievement of control comes at the conclusion of the following or completion stage (Tib. dzok-rim) and is synonymous with Buddhahood. (See note 32 for detailed explanation.)

25 The three bodies of a Buddha are the Dharmakaya (Tib. chö-ku) or Truth Body, the Samboghakaya (Tib. long-ku) or Complete Enjoyment Body and the Nirmanakaya (Tib. trul-ku) or Emanation Body. The Dharmakaya is formless and represents an enlightened being's undifferentiable union with the all-pervasive sphere of emptiness (not a single dimension or place as such, but as the ultimate reality of all phenomena that which abides throughout). On the other hand, the two remaining bodies are known as form bodies. The Samboghakaya is a spontaneous projection from the Dharmakaya, produced by a Buddha's wishes to help sentient beings. It appears to train advanced Bodhisattvas in the higher pure lands and is known as The Complete Enjoyment Body because of its pure nature. Nirmanakaya are lower level physical forms of a Buddha (sometimes distinguished by 32 major and 80 minor marks) which can manifest in the human realm when times are suitable to teach the Dharma. While the Dharmakaya is the direct product of a Buddha's insight into the ultimate nature of reality—his wisdom—the two form bodies are a result of the altruistic motivation to help others. As a result, they are infinite in number, manifesting throughout time and space whenever and wherever there are beings capable of being led towards liberation. Therefore, though the form bodies are produced by a Buddha's compassion, they only appear contingent on the merit of others.

26 Trainee means all those who are training in the practices which lead to enlightenment.

27 Manjushri (Tib. Jam-pel) is the Bodhisattva of Infinite Wisdom. Maitreya (Tib. Jam-pa) is the next (no. 5) of the 1000 Universal or Teaching Buddhas, who will appear during this world's twenty intermediate aeons of abiding. He is currently dwelling in the Tushita Heaven, where the last historical Buddha-Shakyamuni—left him in charge of teaching the Bodhisattva-host, there assembled.

28 Tulku in Tibetan literally means Emanation Body. In general usage, it refers to any great saint or sage who, having obtained the ability not to reincarnate, does so

voluntarily for the benefit of others. Such a being need not have obtained Buddhahood, but must at the least, have gained sufficient realization of emptiness to determine the place and circumstances under which he will be reborn. This ability is achieved at the level of the path of seeing, the third of the five paths of spiritual attainment leading to enlightenment.

29   Shariputra and Maudgalyayana were the Buddha's two principal disciples.

30   Clear light (Tib. o-sel) is the term used to describe the basic entity of the mind from the viewpoint of the experiencing consciousness. Objectively speaking, clear light is emptiness itself. Subjectively, it is the subtlest consciousness realizing emptiness.

31   The vajra-like samadhi of a learner is the final degree of insight prior to obtaining Buddhahood, reached at the end of the 10th Bodhisattva stage. Vajra (Tib. dorjé) means adamantine or diamond-like and in this context describes that state of a learner (one who has not yet become a Buddha) which cannot be damaged or obstructed.

32   There are eight principal layers of consciousness which comprise the subtler levels of a human being's mind. Ordinarily, we experience all eight on numerous occasions during the day. They pass in such rapid succession, however, that only an advanced practitioner can recognize their existence. The main times of their occurrence—in which they unfold and re-emerge from the most coarse to the most subtle degree and back—are on going to sleep, on waking, at the start and finish of individual dreams, while fainting and sneezing, during sexual orgasm and at death. The most subtle of the eight—the basic nature of the mind itself—is clear light. The most coarse, just underlying our normal waking consciousness is called mirage-like. Taking this as no. 1 and progressing inwardly to clear light no. 8, the others are 2) smoke-like appearance 3) like fireflies 4) like the steady flame of a butter lamp 5) the mind of radiant white appearance 6) the mind of radiant red or orange increase 7) the mind of radiant black near-attainment and finally 8) clear light. The last four are known as the four empties and are those states referred to by the Dalai Lama.

It is the particular purpose of Annutara or Highest Yoga Tantra to facilitate the meditator's awareness of and eventual control over all eight states. One endeavors to obtain such control during the stage of completion. (see note #24) Technically, a fully enlightened being or Buddha, is someone who can remain in the most fundamental level of consciousness—clear light—without being compelled backwards by past karma and mental obscurations (Sans. klesha; Tib. nyon-mong) into the coarser states. From such a position the Buddha can then emanate forms directly, without having to adopt the less developed states of awareness which normally give rise to physical manifestations. The techniques used for becoming aware of and subsequently controlling the eight consciousnesses involve manipulation through various means of the ten inner winds coursing through the 72,000 psychic channels (Sans. nadis; Tib. rtsa) which regulate the human nervous system. These winds form the physical supports upon which the various states of consciousness are mounted. As they are brought into the central channel (Tib. u-ma) the different consciousnesses occur, final liberation being obtained at the conclusion of the completion stage when the four minds of appearance are passed through and the first three do not reoccur. For those who have achieved a good degree of proficiency in such practices, the time of death is looked forward to as a rare opportunity. At that time, there is no need to meditatively induce the eight states, as they occur within the dying person's awareness one by one on being severed from their physical supports. An advanced yogi can utilize this by remaining forcibly within the clear light when it dawns; not being cast back into another rebirth, but arising instead in an illusory body.

33 Tibetan medicine recognizes three groups of five humors each which make up the metabolism of a human body: wind, bile and phlegm. The five major winds or currents of energy are said to be light, rough, cold and energetic; the five types of bile are oily, acrid and hot; the five phlegms; cool, heavy, gentle and sticky.

34 Samantabhadra (Tib. Kun-tu-sang-po) literally means "In All Ways Good." Here it refers not to a particular being, but the basic entity of our minds: clear light.

35 Chandrakirti was one of the foremost proponents of the Prasangika-Madhyamika School of Mahayana Buddhism.

36 Conventional truth (Sans. samvrtisatya; Tib. kun-dzop-den-pa) refers to the relative nature of phenomena. According to the Prasangika-Madhyamika School (herein described), things exist conventionally as dependent-arisings. This is to say that nothing exists in and of itself, under its own power or by its own nature. Rather, entities arise in dependence upon causes and conditions as well as their parts. Relatively then, things do exist, but as they lack independence and are not self-originated they are ultimately non-existent. Hence, the middle path taught by the Buddha, (from which the Madhyamika School derives its name) falls to neither the extreme of existence nor non-existence, and in so doing goes beyond both to recognize the two truths as one entity.

37 Dharmata (Tib. chö-nyid) is another term for the ultimate nature of phenomena.

38 The red and white constituents (Tib. tig-le-mar-po and tig-le-kar-po) are subtle material essences held (in tantric practice) to be the principal controlling and generative elements of the human form. Tig-le in Tibetan means drop (Sans. bindu); the name most often given these. The red drop embodies the female components of a person; the white, the male. They originate respectively from one's mother and father at the time of conception, from which point they form the first stage in the growth of the body in the womb. As the embryo develops, they gradually disengage. In the fully matured form, the red drop occupies a place above the groin; the white at the top of the head. At death the former ascends up the central channel while the latter descends. They reunite in the region of the heart (where the primary mind dwells), their meeting marking the collapse of the final support between consciousness and the body and the culmination of the death process. At this time secretions will emerge from both nostrils indicating that the person has died. (In some cases, it can be as long as three days before this occurs.)

39 Misconceiving things to inherently exist produces both karmic seeds for future misconception (Sans. kleshavarana; Tib. nyon-drib) as well as an underlying predisposition, or latent tendency (Sans. jneyavarana; Tib. she-drib) to do so. The actual seeds or causes of misconception are eliminated—along with the afflictive emotions—by the view of emptiness at the level of the eighth Bodhisattva stage. The predispositions or latencies, however, are not. It is these predispositions which give rise to the continued appearance of inherently existent objects, even though the actual conception of them

as such has been destroyed. Thus, the view of emptiness needs to be augmented or strengthened to a point where the predispositions are eradicated, permitting one to view both a conventional object and its ultimate state of emptiness at once. Such a view is identical with omniscience. It is the appearance of concrete existence (produced by the predispositions) which obstructs the mind from knowing all things throughout time and space—just as a wall blocks the view behind it. There is only one method for overcoming the predisposition to view things as truly existent: compassionate means (Sans. upaya; Tib. thab). The altruistic motivation, conjoined with its resulting deeds, has the power to boost the view of emptiness so that the obstructions to omniscience are overcome and the two truths cognized simultaneously. Due to this, a Hinayana Arhat may have obtained freedom from cyclic existence (based on a correct view of emptiness) but because he or she lacks the motivation to help others—such as that possessed by a Bodhisattva—they cannot reach the state of Buddhahood. Nevertheless, Mahayanists maintain that such beings will eventually recognize their limitations and commence to train in developing great compassion.

40 The three types of Arhats (Tib. Dra-jom-pa) or Foe Destroyers—so called because they have destroyed the afflictive obscurations—are 1) a Shravaka (Tib. Nyen-tö) or Listener; one who obtains liberation for his or her sake only; 2) a Pratyekabuddha (Tib. Rang-gyel) or Solitary Realizer, one who obtains liberation for his own sake and in his last life does not rely on a teacher; 3) a Buddha (Tib. Sang-gye) who achieves full enlightenment for the sake of all sentient beings. While the first two ranks may be obtained by following the Hinayana paths, the rank of Buddhahood is only reached by engaging in the Mahayana.

41 Compassionate means (Sans. upaya; Tib. thab) and wisdom (Sans. prajna; Tib. she-rab) are the two mainstays of Mahayana practice. By the accumulation of merit through altruistic deeds, one purifies negative karma, thereby directly removing obstacles to the attainment of wisdom. On the other hand, wisdom or realization of the two truths, enhances one's compassion by destroying the cherishing of a non-existent self.

42 The three vehicles or avenues to enlightenment are those of the Shravaka, Pratyekabuddha and Bodhisattva (often referred to as the Perfection Vehicle). The first two are Hinayana, the last, Mahayana.

43 The six perfections (Sans. paramita; Tib. pa-rol-tu-chin-pa) are the distinctive features of the general Mahayana. They are 1) giving (Sans. dāna; Tib. jin-ba); 2) morality (Sans. shila; Tib. tsul-trim); 3) patience (Sans. kshanti; Tib. zö-pa); 4) perseverance (Sans. virya; Tib. tson-dru); 5) meditation (Sans. dhyana; Tib. sam-ten); 6) wisdom (Sans. prajna; Tib. she-rab). By perfecting these six qualities and attainments, a Bodhisattva passes through the five paths and ten stages leading to Buddhahood.

Bibliography

TIBET

1 *My Land And My People: Memoirs of The Dalai Lama,* Potala Publications, 801 2nd Avenue, Suite 703, New York, New York 10017.

2 *Tibet Is My Country:* Thubten Jigme Norbu (Brother of the Dalai Lama) as told to Heinrich Harrer, E. P. Dutton and Company, New York, 1961.

3 *My Life And Lives: The Story of A Tibetan Incarnation* by Rato Khyongla Nawang Losang, E. P. Dutton, New York, 1977.

4 *Tibet: A Political History;* Tsepon W. D. Shakabpa, Yale University Press, 1967.

BUDDHISM

1 *The Wisdom of Tibet Series:* Volume 1: *The Buddhism of Tibet and the Key To The Middle Way* by His Holiness The Dalai Lama; translated by Jeffrey Hopkins and Lati Rimpoché, Harper and Row Publishers, New York and London.

Volume II: *The Precious Garland And The Song Of The Four Mindfulnesses,* Nagarjuna and the Seventh Dalai Lama, translated by Jeffrey Hopkins and Lati Rimpoché; George, Allen and Unwin, Ltd., London.

Volume III: *Tantra In Tibet,* Tsongkapa, translated and edited by Jeffrey Hopkins; George, Allen and Unwin, Ltd., London.

2 *The Opening of the Wisdom Eye* by His Holiness The Dalai Lama, Theosophical Publishing House, Wheaton, Illinois.

3 *Death, Intermediate State and Rebirth in Tibetan Buddhism,* translated by Jeffrey Hopkins; Rider and Company, London.

4 *Tibetan Tradition of Mental Development;* Geshé Ngawang Dhargey, Library of Tibetan Works and Archives, Gangchen Kyishong, Dharamsala H. P., India.